New

DIRECTIONS

WRITTEN AND RESEARCHED BY

Samantha Cook

ROUGH GUIDES

NEW YORK • LONDON • DELHI

www.roughguides.com

Contents

Introduction to

New Orleans

Proudly apart from the rest of the United States, New Orleans is intoxicating and addictive, the product of a dizzying jumble of influences. It's a place where people dance at funerals and hold parties during hurricanes, where some of the world's finest musicians make ends meet busking on street corners, and fabulous Creole cuisine is dished up in hole-in-the-wall dives. There's a wistfulness, too, in the peeling, ice-cream–toned facades of the old French Quarter – site of the original settlement – in the filigree cast-iron balconies overgrown with lush ferns and fragrant jasmine, and in the cemeteries, or "Cities of the Dead," lined with crumbling above-ground tombs. Doubtless New Orleans' melancholy air – and perhaps its joie de vivre, too – owes much to the city's perilous geography. Set largely below sea level and exposed to the devastating storms that career through the Gulf of Mexico, the city could be washed or blasted away in an instant.

▼ French Quarter street performer

▼ Jazz in Tremé

Founded by the French in 1718 on the swampy flood plain of the lower Mississippi River, and today spreading back as far as Lake Pontchartrain, New Orleans is almost entirely surrounded by water, which has always both isolated it from the interior and connected it to the outside world. By the time the Americans bought it, in the Louisiana Purchase of 1803, New Orleans was a cosmopolitan city whose ethnically diverse population had mingled to create a distinctive Creole culture. In the 1800s, its importance as a port brought in the smugglers, gamblers, prostitutes, and pirates who gave it the decadent "sin city" notoriety it retains today. Since then, more and more visitors, among them an inordinate number of artists, writers, and sundry bohemians, have poured in; many found themselves staying, unable to shake the place from their system.

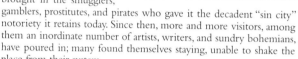

▼ St Louis Cathedral

With its subtropical climate, Latin-influenced architecture, black majority population, its voodoo worshippers, and its long-held carnival traditions, New Orleans is often called the northernmost Caribbean city. The pace of life is slow here, while the sybaritic vices are relished – no more so than during the many festivals, especially world-famous Mardi Gras, during which real life is put on hold as businessmen and bus-boys alike are swept along by an increasingly frenzied season of parties, street parades, and masquerade balls.

▶ Frenchmen Street nightlife

▼ Mardi Gras beads

When to visit

New Orleans has a subtropical **climate**, with warm temperatures, high humidity, and heavy rainfall. The city stays pretty full year-round, but the peak **tourist seasons** are Mardi Gras – which starts on Twelfth Night and builds up in intensity until Mardi Gras itself, the day before Ash Wednesday – and Jazz Fest, held at the end of April and the start of May. Both, along with the French Quarter Festival, occur in **spring**, which is a pleasant, sunny time to visit. However, the humidity is already building up by then, and there are occasional heavy rains. The torpid months between May and September, plagued by debilitating heat and humidity, count as **off-season**; prices may be lower and crowds thinner, but for good reason. From May to November the city is at risk from the **hurricanes** that sweep through the Gulf; New Orleans can be seriously affected by a tropical storm landing anywhere along the coast.

Climate-wise, **fall** is the best time to visit: October especially tends to be sunny, warm, and relatively dry, though the nights can be chilly. Even **winter** days don't usually get too cold; the nights, however, are another matter, cursed by the bone-biting damp that creeps in from the river.

New Orleans
AT A GLANCE

to the CBD (Central Business District). This was the early "American sector," settled by Anglo-Americans after the Louisiana Purchase in 1803. Today, dominated by offices, hotels, and banks, it also features the revitalizing Warehouse District, studded with galleries and museums.

▲ Lafitte's Blacksmith Shop

▼ Dining in the CBD

FRENCH QUARTER

Most tourists head first for the hauntingly lovely, battered old French Quarter, site of the original city, established in 1718. Centering on lively Jackson Square and bordering the Mississippi, the Quarter's quirky combination of ravishing Creole architecture, fabulous restaurants, and eccentric street life soon proves irresistible.

THE CBD AND WAREHOUSE DISTRICT

Leaving the Quarter and crossing the broad, appealingly old-fashioned Canal Street brings you

THE MISSISSIPPI RIVER

Whether relaxing on a lazy paddle-wheeler jazz cruise, or watching the sun set from a bench on the Moonwalk, you can't fail but be

▼ The Mississippi River

awestruck by the majestic, romantic presence of this mighty river.

TREMÉ

Music permeates everything in this low-rent, historic African-American neighborhood, from the performances at Louis Armstrong Park and the neighborhood jazz clubs, to the lively parades where umbrella-twirling dancers and blasting brass bands lead crowds of hundreds through the streets just as they have for centuries.

FAUBOURG MARIGNY

Oak-shaded Esplanade Avenue, lined with crumbling Italianate mansions, separates the Quarter from the funky Faubourg Marigny, an artsy district of ramshackle Creole cottages. Predominantly residential, the Faubourg features a string of excellent bars, clubs, and restaurants, especially along Frenchmen Street.

▼ St Charles Avenue

▲ Faubourg Marigny street scene

GARDEN DISTRICT

Perhaps the most taxing thing you'll do in New Orleans is head out on the historic St Charles streetcar to the residential Garden District, where gorgeous old mansions and dark green shrubs weighed down by fat magnolia blossoms squat in the shadow of centuries-old live oaks.

Ideas

The big six

New Orleans is a city of sensual experiences. To truly enjoy it, you'll need to slip into the indolent way of life, rejecting an itinerary of museum-hopping in favor of a stroll around the French Quarter, a leisurely cruise on the Mississippi, or simply kicking back in Jackson Square. Nights are long and decadent, a whirl of fine food, long cold drinks at distinctive bars, and an indigenous live music scene to rival any in the world.

▲ Drinking

Decadent, dreamy, down-at-heel, and in love with life: New Orleans is one of the world's great drinking cities. First stop should be the *Napoleon House*, the quintessential New Orleans bar.

P.75 ▶ CHARTRES STREET

▲ St Charles streetcar

Take a break from the Quarter by hopping on the St Charles streetcar, a national historic monument that rumbles its way along St Charles Avenue, the city's showpiece boulevard, to the tranquil Garden District.

P.136 ▶ THE GARDEN DISTRICT

▲ Eating out

Whether you want to dine on Creole cuisine in a ravishing subtropical courtyard or chow down on fried chicken at a hole-in-the-wall, gluttony in New Orleans is always rewarded.

P.195 ▶ ESSENTIALS

▲ Parading

From the mighty floats of Mardi Gras, through the umbrella-twirling dancers and roof-raising brass bands of Tremé's Second Line parades, to quirky local barcrawls held at Halloween, New Orleans just loves a parade.

P.114 ▶ RAMPART STREET AND TREMÉ

▲ Cruising on the Mississippi River

There's an undeniable romance in taking a cruise in an old paddleboat along Ole Man River, one of the world's greatest waterways – and it's a great way to grab some breezes on those sultry New Orleans afternoons.

P.99 ▶ THE MISSISSIPPI RIVER

▼ Brass bands in Jackson Square

Enjoy the brass band buskers, whose improvised, euphoric, and highly danceable jazz/R&B/carnival sound captures the heart and soul of a city defined by its live music.

P.51 ▶ JACKSON SQUARE

Creole cuisine

The atmosphere alone at New Orleans' swanky old-guard restaurants, serving haute Creole cuisine in elegant surroundings, makes it well worth splashing out. Not all of them are as expensive as you might imagine, especially at lunchtime.

▲ Galatoire's

Traditional New Orleans style is alive and well in this fabulous old French-Creole place; its unlikely position among the tawdry bars of Bourbon Street only gives it more quirky cachet.

P.90 ▶ BOURBON STREET

▲ Dooky Chase's

A beacon of creativity in a blighted neighborhood, *Dooky's* serves high-class black Creole cuisine, including one of the city's best lunchtime buffets, to a dressed-up, appreciative clientele.

P.160 ▶ MID-CITY

▲ Girod's Bistro

Heading through the *Napoleon House* courtyard brings you to this lesser-known gem, where delicious, robust Mediterranean-Creole food is served in the most romantic of surroundings.

▼ Tujague's

The food may not be the best in town, but dining at this venerable Creole restaurant is an unmissable only-in-New Orleans experience that has barely changed since the 1800s.

▲ Jacques Imo's

Creole cuisine gets funky at this youthful, city favourite. Colorful *Jacques'* is *the* place to fill up before dancing to the ReBirth Brass Band at the *Maple Leaf* on Tuesday nights.

▶ Commander's Palace

With its superb food and impeccable service, New Orleans' showpiece restaurant has more than earned its worldwide reputation; it's not too stuffy, either, with lovely courtyards and a popular, affordable Sunday brunch.

Jazz

The music the city can call its own, jazz is still an evolving art form in New Orleans, and you'll be spoiled for choice for places to hear it here. Local, world-class musicians play regularly – with a preponderance of staggeringly good pianists – and national artists often stop here while touring. In addition, the new breed of youthful brass bands have brought a joyous, chaotic energy to the local jazz scene.

▲ Palm Court Jazz Café

Slightly cheesy, but lots of fun, with a nightly roster of top-notch traditional bands in a high-spirited supper-club atmosphere.

P.68 ▸ DECATUR STREET

▲ Jazz Museum

Wonderfully illuminating, this museum is packed with affecting artifacts, from time-worn musical instruments through photos and old playbills.

P.62 ▸ DECATUR STREET

▼ Brass bands

Ragtag groups of musicians blast out a joyful, improvised, and eminently danceable sound that goes down as well in the student bars as in the Second Line parades.

P.114 ▶ RAMPART STREET AND TREMÉ

▼ Preservation Hall

You can't say you like traditional jazz and not make the pilgrimage to The Hall. The crowds, the shabby setting, the lack of air-conditioning, toilets, seating, or bar – they all add to the fun.

P.93 ▶ BOURBON STREET

▲ Visitor Center

This airy space offers a daily program of live music, workshops, seminars, and movies – all for free.

P.62 ▶ DECATUR STREET

Mardi Gras

Businessmen donning wigs, ermine-trimmed robes, and bejeweled scepters; satirical, shambolic parades weaving through the French Quarter; tits out on Bourbon Street – New Orleans' unique carnival, which consumes the entire city for a full six weeks, is crazy, life-affirming, and just a little disarming.

▲ Masking and costumes

Don't even think of coming to Mardi Gras and not dressing up. Costumes, which can be thrown together in a day, celebrate creativity, humor, and darkness in equal measure.

P.162 ▸ MARDI GRAS

▲ Bourbon Street

The heart of gay carnival, Bourbon is bedlam during Mardi Gras. It also hosts the amazing Bourbon Street costume awards, and an essential stop on Fat Tuesday.

P.171 ▸ MARDI GRAS

▲ Superkrewe parades

The superkrewe parades are the highlight of official carnival, with their vast, beautifully designed floats, their ear-splitting brass bands, and the generosity of the throws they fling into the crowds.

P.166 ▶ MARDI GRAS

▼ Barkus

Corny themes and dreadful puns abound at canine carnival, with thousands of dolled-up doggies trotting proudly through the Quarter in their own special parade.

P.166 ▶ MARDI GRAS

▲ Mardi Gras Indians

In a spiritual tradition unchanged for more than a century, Mardi Gras morning sees rival tribes hit the streets to parade, sing, and show off their amazing feathered costumes.

P.166 ▶ MARDI GRAS

▶ St Ann Walking Parade

Everyone's welcome to tag along on the dazzling St Ann parade, an artsy, semi-drunken ensemble devoted to all things bizarre and beautiful – just make sure you dress up.

P.171 ▶ MARDI GRAS

The French Quarter

The heartbreakingly beautiful French Quarter, where New Orleans began, is battered and bohemian, decaying and vibrant. Today, it's the spiritual core of the city, its fanciful cast-iron balconies, hidden courtyards, and time-stained stucco buildings exerting a fascination that has long caught the imaginations of artists and writers.

▲ Street musicians

You'll find excellent makeshift bands on street corners throughout the Quarter, playing superb roots music – blues, country, bluegrass, jazz – all day long.

P.77 ▸ ROYAL STREET

▲ Bourbon Street

Grab a potent cocktail to go and take a nighttime stroll down world-renowned Bourbon Street. Among the tacky girly clubs, noisy karaoke bars, and rowdy gay discos, you'll even come across some fine old-time restaurants and bars.

P.86 ▸ BOURBON STREET

▼ Café du Monde

The place to snack on sugary beignets (donuts) and café au lait made with chicory, this iconic coffeehouse is as good a place to start the day as to end a long night.

P.58 ▶ JACKSON SQUARE

▲ Lower Decatur Street

Bohemian, funky, and a little grungy, Lower Decatur Street boasts a really good crop of quirky vintage and rummage stores.

P.60 ▶ DECATUR STREET

▶ Ironwork balconies

With their intricate filigree tracery, the Quarter's elegant cast-iron balconies have defined its haunting beauty since the mid-nineteenth century.

P.77 ▶ ROYAL STREET

▼ Jackson Square

The hub of the Quarter buzzes with live performers, tarot readers, and street art, such as the works of Big Al Taplet, pictured here.

P.51 ▶ JACKSON SQUARE

Bars

As befits its image as a hard-drinking, late-partying town, New Orleans has dozens of truly great bars. Locals love to drink, and tourists, it seems, even more so, and there are more than enough places to cater to all of them. Whether you want to sip a Sazerac under the stars or select ear-blasting R&B on a jukebox, you'll find your niche here. For the legalities of drinking in New Orleans, see p.196.

▲ Columns Hotel Bar

Faded grandeur and shabby opulence abound at this gorgeous old hotel bar. On warm evenings find a seat on the huge columned veranda and watch as the streetcar sweeps by under the majestic oak canopy.

P.151 ▸ UPTOWN

▲ Port of Call

Neighborhood haunt that's always lively with a rowdy mix of Quarterites, Faubourg hipsters, and happy tourists chowing down on some of the best burgers in town.

P.110 ▸ FAUBOURG MARIGNY AND BYWATER

▲ Saturn Bar

Cats, dogs, junk, car parts – be careful what you stumble over in this excessively eccentric ragbag of a place.

P.110 ▶ FAUBOURG MARIGNY AND BYWATER

▼ R-Bar

With its cool vibe, pool sharks, rocking jukebox, and groovy decor, the *R-Bar* is a stalwart of the youthful Faubourg scene.

P.110 ▶ FAUBOURG MARIGNY AND BYWATER

▲ Ernie K-Doe's Mother-in-Law Lounge

Late R&B legend Ernie, the self-styled "Emperor of the World," lives on in this extraordinary shrine, presided over by his widow, Antoinette, as well as sundry friends, neighbors, and hipsters.

P.119 ▶ RAMPART STREET AND TREMÉ

Costumes and masking

New Orleanians love to dress up, whatever the occasion. Scores of shops sell cheap masks, feather boas, and fancy hats to satisfy exhibitionist impulses, but for serious costuming – at Mardi Gras or Halloween – you should head for the quirky specialist shops, many of them vintage stores, geared up towards outfitting you in marvelous gear. Even during off-season, they're worth a browse.

▲ Vieux Carré Hair Shop

Whether you're after a Heidi wig or a Hitler moustache, false eyelashes, or a false ass, this charmingly kitschy family-run store won't fail to win you over.

P.149 ▸ UPTOWN

▲ Little Shop of Fantasy

Several cuts above your three-masks-for-a-dollar stores on Decatur Street, with weird and beautiful designer masks that are almost too good to wear.

P.64 ▸ DECATUR STREET

▼ Fifi Mahony's

Shocking-pink eyelashes and glitter lipstick, stick-on jewels, and fluorescent hairpieces – every camp and fabulous accessory you could dream of is here.

P.82 ▶ ROYAL STREET

▼ Uptown Costume and Dancewear Company

Want an Elvis jumpsuit or a Donald Rumsfeld latex head? Look no further.

P.149 ▶ UPTOWN

▲ Funky Monkey

The vintage gladrags in this Magazine Street store, including old Mardi Gras garb, are perfect if you're planning to throw together a unique carnival costume.

P.140 ▶ THE GARDEN DISTRICT

Hotels and guesthouses

While there are scores of chain hotels and swanky high-rise towers in New Orleans, avoid those, and head instead for the quaint and quirky guesthouses that give you a genuine taste of the city's character. You don't need to slum it, either – many of them are special places where, if you don't mind a bit of Victorian plumbing, you'll leave feeling pampered and relaxed.

▲ Olivier House

This gorgeous old Creole townhouse features a warren of lovely rooms, a ravishing court-yard, and a wonderful location in the heart of the Quarter.

P.178 ▶ ACCOMMODATION

▲ Royal Street Inn

Enjoy bed and beverages at this funky, good-value place above one of the Faubourg's hippest bars.

P.180 ▶ ACCOMMODATION

▼ Josephine Guesthouse

New Orleans elegance, quirkiness, and love of the good life are all wrapped up into one gorgeous package here.

P.181 ▶ ACCOMMODATION

▲ Cornstalk Hotel

With its landmark cast-iron fence, wrap-around balconies, and pretty garden, the *Cornstalk* is one of the Quarter's showpiece guesthouses. Take breakfast on the veranda and watch passers-by gawk.

P.178 ▶ ACCOMMODATION

▼ Lafitte Guesthouse

On a quiet section of Bourbon Street, this gay-friendly guesthouse is a cut above, with elegant rooms and a fine attention to detail.

P.178 ▶ ACCOMMODATION

▲ Hotel Maison de Ville

Tennessee Williams stayed here. And Elizabeth Taylor. It's simply divine, darling.

P.178 ▶ ACCOMMODATION

House museums

Whether you're interested in vernacular architecture, decorative arts, or simply want a sense of how daily life in New Orleans has changed – or, in many cases, remained unchanged – over the centuries, get behind the closed doors of one of the city's many house museums.

▲ Hermann-Grima House

Come here for an authentic re-creation of middle-class Creole life in antebellum New Orleans; try to time your visit to coincide with the weekly Creole cooking demonstrations.

P.86 ▶ BOURBON STREET

▲ Gallier House

Lively tours at this Creole townhouse – the inspiration for Lestat's home in *Interview with the Vampire* – bring nineteenth-century New Orleans to life.

P.81 ▶ ROYAL STREET

▲ Pitot House

Set on the banks of Bayou St John, this picturesque West Indies-style plantation home offers fascinating historical tours and is well worth a trip out of the Quarter.

P.155 ▸ MID-CITY

▶ Madame John's Legacy

Early West Indies-style residence holds an intriguing display detailing the house's changes in fortune as well as a treasure-trove of folk art in the tranquil upstairs rooms.

P.80 ▸ ROYAL STREET

▼ Beauregard-Keyes House

This notable antebellum home will appeal to fans of decorative arts and of the historical romances of Frances Parkinson Keyes.

P.71 ▸ CHARTRES STREET

Shopping

In New Orleans, where megamalls play second fiddle to small, stylish stores, shopping is a lot of fun. Though big spenders may want to head for the world-class antique stores along Royal and Magazine streets, there are plenty of bargains to be had in the specialist record and used book stores, and many stylish little boutiques specializing in the city's dramatic, romantic, and rather nostalgic style.

▼ Lucullus

Satisfy your most gluttonous kitchenware desires in this unusual antique store, which sells vintage pots and pans, armoires, butter knives, and china coffee cups.

P.72 ▶ CHARTRES STREET

▼ The French Market

Whether you're after gator on a stick, fresh seafood, or bottles of lethal hot sauce, these venerable market arcades are touristy yet fun.

P.61 ▶ DECATUR STREET

▼ Trashy Diva

New Orleans' distinctively sexy, vintage style infuses everything here from the drop-dead gorgeous corsets to the oversized velvet corsages.

P.73 ▶ CHARTRES STREET

▼ Louisiana Music Factory

This French Quarter institution sells the finest of New Orleans and roots music on vinyl and CD, and, best of all, hosts regular free live performances from fantastic local bands.

P.64 ▶ DECATUR STREET

▲ Le Monde Creole

The place to come for quirky, shabby-chic Creole-related books, music, and gifts, with a stunning tropical courtyard to boot.

P.83 ▶ ROYAL STREET

Coffeehouses

New Orleans has traditionally been *the* American city for coffee, and today locals drink twice the national average. The city's smoky chicory coffee, particularly good with a sugary *beignet*, dates back to the early European colonists, who stretched out their precious coffee supplies by adding the ground root of the endive plant. Most coffeehouses serve snacks and pastries, too, and many will rustle up breakfasts and light lunches.

TEAS AND MILKS
HOT TEAS
HOT HERBAL TEAS
ICED TEAS
HOT CHAI
ICED CHAI
HOT CHOCOLATE
STEAMERS
COLD MILK
COLD CHOCOLATE MILK

▲ CC's Community Coffeehouse

Settle down on a plump leather armchair by the open French windows and order a creamy Mochasippi – you might just stay here all day.

P.83 ▸ ROYAL STREET

▲ Croissant d'Or

A tranquil favorite in the Quarter, serving café au lait, light lunches, and amazing cakes in an old, tiled ice-cream parlor.

P.83 ▸ ROYAL STREET

▲ Rue de la Course

With branches around the city, the biggest *Rue* is the best, buzzing at the weekends with earnest students and groovy shoppers taking a break from the stores on Magazine Street.

P.141 ▸ THE GARDEN DISTRICT

▼ Z'otz

Young artists, avant-garde musicians, and all manner of pierced poets sip strong coffees, crazy-flavored teas, and herbal hookahs in this wildly boho 24hr joint.

P.107 ▸ FAUBOURG MARIGNY
AND BYWATER

▲ La Marquise

Scrumptious French pastries and a tower of froth on your cappuccino – plus a sweet, shady courtyard to retreat to.

P.73 ▸ CHARTRES STREET

Architecture

New Orleans' minor league status, in commercial terms, has protected it from the modernization that has ripped out the old hearts of wealthier cities, allowing it to hold on to its distinctive architectural character. That, with a combination of conservatism, nostalgia, and a highly active preservation movement, ensures that the city abounds with styles from Creole vernacular through French and Spanish colonial to Greek Revival.

▲ Greek Revival

New Orleans' antebellum Greek Revival styling reached its apex in the Garden District, where fat columns, grand entranceways, and bold rows of windows are set off by lush, landscaped gardens.

P.134 ▶ THE GARDEN DISTRICT

▲ Shotgun houses

Composed of a single row of rooms opening onto each other, shotgun houses are so named because you could shoot a bullet from the front door to the back without it hitting a thing.

P.94 ▶ ABOVE BOURBON STREET

▲ Early West-Indies style

The 1730 Madame John's Legacy is notable for its deep wraparound gallery, dramatically steep pitched roof, and narrow dormer windows.

P.53 ▶ ROYAL STREET

▶ Italianate

In the 1860s, the romantic Italianate style swept the city; exquisite cast-iron balconies and decorative detailing soon superseded the simpler, more austere Greek Revival style.

P.134 ▶ THE GARDEN DISTRICT

◀ Creole cottages

Originating in the late 1700s, these simple structures predate the fine filigree balconies that are so identified with the French Quarter and help create a streetscape little changed since Creole days.

P.57 ▶ JACKSON SQUARE

New Orleans food

A gourmand's dream, the Crescent City attracts many visitors for its restaurants alone, and locals will spend hours arguing about where to get the fattest po-boy, the plumpest raw oysters, or the tastiest gumbo. The food itself, defined as Creole, is a spicy, substantial blend of French, Spanish, African, Italian, Caribbean, and Cajun cuisine, mixed up with other influences including Native American and German. For a glossary of helpful food terms, see p.195.

▲ Oysters and crawfish

Seafood fans won't want to miss New Orleans' famously plump raw oysters, shucked and slurped at marble-topped counters throughout the city, and its crawfish, which are delicious cooked simply in a spicy stock.

P.89 ▶ BOURBON STREET

▲ Shrimp

Served in everything from omelets to bisques, with a rémoulade, or étouffé over rice, shrimp is a mainstay of any self-respecting New Orleans menu.

P.90 ▶ BOURBON STREET

▲ Po-boy

In true New Orleans style, the vast sub-like sandwiches known as po-boys are overstuffed with anything from oysters to French fries.

P.65 ▸ DECATUR STREET

▸ Muffuletta

Monster Italian sandwiches, piled high with smoked meats, cheese, and garlicky olive dressing. Join the lines at the old *Central Grocery* and take one down to the river for a picnic.

P.65 ▸ THE MISSISSIPPI RIVER

▾ Gumbo and jambalaya

They may not look much, but these Creole favorites, packed with shrimp, chicken, spicy sausage, or vegetables (or all four) are tasty and substantial, whether dished up in corner delis or swanky restaurants.

P.195 ▸ ESSENTIALS

Spooky New Orleans

New Orleans has a strange love affair with all things morbid. Repeatedly devastated by diseases and epidemics, its earliest settlers buried their loved ones in European-style above-ground cemeteries, atmospheric, eerie "Cities of the Dead" that have become major tourist attractions. Contributing to this spooky aura, immigrants from Haiti and West Africa have upheld their voodoo traditions, and this syncretic religion permeates the city today.

▲ St Louis No. 3

A skyline of delicate marble angels looks over you as you wander the aisles of this peaceful burial ground.

P.154 ▶ MID-CITY

▲ The Historic Voodoo Museum

Shrines, shrunken heads, and hypnotic drum music – this French Quarter museum plays on the more lurid aspects of voodoo while managing to pack in a lot of useful information at the same time.

P.87 ▶ BOURBON STREET

▲ Lafayette No. 1 Cemetery

In the heart of the Garden District, this picturesque cemetery is one of the most appealing of New Orleans' "cities of the dead."

P.140 ▶ THE GARDEN DISTRICT

▼ Voodoo Spiritual Temple

Find out all about the history and practice of this misunderstood religion at an authentic voodoo temple.

P.88 ▶ RAMPART STREET AND TREMÉ

▶ Marie Laveau's Tomb

The resting place of New Orleans' voodoo queen, in St Louis Cemetery No. 1, is a holy place for the city's voodooists, and always surrounded by offerings and treats.

P.115 ▶ RAMPART STREET AND TREMÉ

Live music

New Orleans is truly one of the best places in the world to hear live music. From the shambling, joyous brass bands to international names like Dr John, music remains integral to the Crescent City. Year-round, though especially during the festivals, the variety and quality of what's on offer – jazz, of course, but also New Orleans' own carnival-tinged R&B, plus funk, blues, Latin, Cajun, zydeco, Mardi Gras Indian music, gospel, and more – is staggering.

▲ Kermit Ruffins at Vaughan's

If it's Thursday night, everyone's heading for *Vaughan's*, a friendly neighborhood bar where consummate trumpet stylist Kermit Ruffins blows up a storm.

P.111 ▶ FAUBOURG MARIGNY AND BYWATER

▲ Rock'n'Bowl

Only in New Orleans – a bowling alley, bar, and dance hall all in one. Their fast, furious, and steamy zydeco nights dare you not to dance.

P.161 ▶ MID-CITY

▼ ReBirth at the Maple Leaf Bar

This old bar is pure New Orleans, with a great roster of local roots music. Tuesday nights, the phenomenal ReBirth Brass Band keeps the crowds dancing till dawn.

P.152 ▶ UPTOWN

▲ Donna's

A down-home barbecue joint dishing up the best in local brass band music, *Donna's* is the only place to be on a Monday night, when drummer Bob French hosts a riotous, convivial jazz jam.

P.118 ▶ RAMPART STREET AND TREMÉ

▼ Frenchmen Street

Latin, tango, reggae, R&B, brass, jazz – Faubourg Marigny's Frenchmen Street is one long stretch of intimate music clubs and friendly bars, many of them free.

P.110 ▶ FAUBOURG MARIGNY AND BYWATER

New Orleans drinks

It is said that the cocktail was invented in New Orleans' French Quarter in the 1790s. Since then, several potent concoctions have been dreamed up in this boozy city, many of them the signature drinks of its classier establishments. Even the humble cup of java doesn't get overlooked – if there's any chance to dowse something in liquor, you can trust New Orleans will take it.

▲ Pimm's Cup

Mysteriously transplanted from England to the French Quarter's *Napoleon House*, the Pimm's Cup, served simply with ice and a slice of cucumber, is a wonderful antidote to those steamy New Orleans afternoons.

P.75 ▶ CHARTRES STREET

▲ Café Brûlot

Rich with spices, orange peel, and brandy, a flaming after-dinner coffee is an unmissable Creole tradition in old-guard New Orleans restaurants like *Galatoire's*.

P.90 ▶ BOURBON STREET

▶ Hurricane

The number one choice for gonna-drink-till-we're-sick out-of-towners, who head straight from the airport to *Pat O'Brien's* on Bourbon Street.

P.91 ▸ BOURBON STREET

▼ Ramos Gin Fizz

Frothy, light, refreshing, and powerful – though it's associated with the *Sazerac Bar*, you'll get better versions at *Tujague's* and the *Napoleon House*.

P.66 ▸ DECATUR STREET

▼ Sazerac cocktail

Head to the famous *Sazerac Bar* and sip one of these classic New Orleans cocktails – made with rye whiskey and Pernod – and watch as the stunning Art Deco surrounds go a little woozy.

P.125 ▸ THE CBD

New Orleans museums

While few come to New Orleans for its high culture, if you need a break from all the music and drinking, there are more than enough worthwhile museums to distract you. Though the major art galleries, the Aquarium of the Americas (p.98), and the National D-Day Museum are world-class, most appealing are those quirky places that give real insights into the city's local history and customs.

▲ The Cabildo

Bang in the heart of the French Quarter, this accessible, illuminating museum of Louisiana history is a model of its kind.

P.53 ▶ JACKSON SQUARE

▲ Historical Pharmacy Museum

Telling the history of medicine with voodoo love potions, glass eyes, Creole quack tonics, and scary-looking drills – plus lots of grisly tales of death and disease for the kiddies.

P.69 ▶ CHARTRES STREET

▼ Presbytère Mardi Gras Museum

As quirky and compelling as carnival itself, the museum is full of fascinating snippets and fabulous costumes.

P.54 ▸ JACKSON SQUARE

▲ Backstreet Cultural Museum

Lovingly put-together celebration of the city's unique street culture and parading traditions, housed in a humble old funeral home in Tremé.

P.116 ▸ RAMPART STREET AND TREMÉ

▼ National D-Day Museum

Daunting in scale and impressively far-reaching in scope, this vast place is always packed with veterans and their families.

P.130 ▸ THE WAREHOUSE DISTRICT

Neighborhood restaurants

If you're on a tight budget, don't despair: one of the great joys of New Orleans' dining scene is the profusion of excellent down-home neighborhood joints. Some of the best food in the city is served in scruffy little dives that you'd barely give a second glance elsewhere.

▲ Frankie and Johnny's

Noisy, friendly, and a haven for fried-food lovers, *Frankie's* is an uptown favorite for Italian-Creole family classics like stuffed artichokes and softshell crabs.

P.150 ▸ UPTOWN

▲ Uglesich's

Arrive early or allow yourself loads of time when you come to this humble-looking sea-food joint. The food is phenomenal, the lines are long, and spirits are high.

P.143 ▸ THE GARDEN DISTRICT

▼ Fiorella's

A cheerful mix of Lower Decatur hipsters, families, and local workers flock to this old joint for phenomenal fried chicken at low, low prices.

P.65 ▸ DECATUR STREET

▲ Acme Oyster House

Super-fresh raw oysters, cold beer, fast-talking waitresses, and a convivial, noisy crowd; you can't help but leave this French Quarter institution feeling happy.

P.89 ▸ BOURBON STREET

▼ Dunbar's

Once a local secret, *Dunbar's* has become famed citywide for its vast portions of Southern/Creole cooking and its gratifyingly low prices.

P.150 ▸ UPTOWN

▲ Casamento's

Step back in time in this gloriously old-fashioned, sparklingly clean temple to oysters in all their guises.

P.149 ▸ UPTOWN

New Orleans festivals

As you'd imagine in this multicultural, hedonistic city, there's far more to New Orleans' festival calendar than Mardi Gras, and the following selection barely does it justice. From devout celebrations of Catholic saint's days to decadent gay extravaganzas, music and food feature prominently, as, of course, do street parades. For a more detailed selection of festivals, see p.192.

▲ Jazz Fest

Locals love to bitch about the crowds and the prices, but this monster music festival, which attracts international acts ranging from gospel to reggae and R&B, is second only to Mardi Gras in the city's festival calendar.

P.193 ▸ ESSENTIALS

▲ Halloween

Another great excuse to don a costume and show off, Halloween sees block parties, wild parades, and bloodcurdling carousing throughout the Quarter and the Faubourg.

P.194 ▸ ESSENTIALS

▲ French Quarter Festival

Splendid free music festival that fills the Quarter for three days with homegrown music and fabulous food stalls. Lower-key than Jazz Fest, it's a local favorite.

P.193 ▸ ESSENTIALS

▼ Southern Decadence

Dissolute and debauched, New Orleans' premier gay festival more than lives up to its name.

P.193 ▸ ESSENTIALS

▶ St Joseph's Day /Super Sunday

Mid-way through Lent, this Italian saint's day sees massive altars of food set up around the city; it's also the only time outside Mardi Gras that the extraordinary Mardi Gras Indians take to the streets to parade.

P.192 ▸ ESSENTIALS

Places

French Quarter: Jackson Square

Ever since its earliest incarnation as the Place d'Armes, a dusty parade ground used for public meetings and executions, Jackson Square has been at the heart of the French Quarter. In 1851 the drill ground was revamped into a landscaped park and renamed for Andrew Jackson, hero of the Battle of New Orleans who went on to become the US president. Bordered by pedestrianized St Peter, Chartres, and St Ann streets, the square is where you'll find the tourist information center (see p.188) and some of the city's major sights: the chic, terraced Pontalba Buildings, their street-level rooms taken up by shops and restaurants; St Louis Cathedral; and, flanking the cathedral like stout body-guards, the Cabildo and Presbytère museums. During the day, everyone passes by at some time or another, weaving their way through the tangle of artists, rain-bow-clad palmists, magicians, shambolic jazz bands, and blues musicians. At night it's more peaceful, with just a few waifs and strays lingering in the shadows cast by the stately, floodlit buildings.

The square

A welcome open space in the congested French Quarter, Jackson Square is bathed in light from the Mississippi, "a worldly sort of light," as Mark Twain put it, that still renders it "brilliant." And with its iron benches, neat lawns, and blaze of flowerbeds, it somehow manages to stay tranquil, despite the streams of photo-snapping tourists, overexcited school groups, waiters on their breaks, and the odd crashed-out casualty. Presiding over them all, an equestrian statue – the first in the nation, constructed by Clark Mills in 1856 – shows Jackson in uncharacteristically jaunty mode, waving his hat. It's a sculptural masterpiece, with the mighty horse, rearing on its hind legs, perfectly balanced on the plinth. The inscription "The Union Must and Shall

▼ ANDREW JACKSON STATUE

Lucky Dogs

Look out for the absurd Lucky Dogs giant hot-dog-shaped carts, set up on the square and on corners throughout the French Quarter. Featured in John Kennedy Toole's quintessential New Orleans tragi-comedy *A Confederacy of Dunces*, in which pompous and repulsive anti-hero Ignatius J. Reilly wreaks havoc through his insalubrious and surreal city, they, and their attendants, have become something of an institution – though in truth the "dogs" themselves are nothing to write home about.

be Preserved" was pointedly added by General "Beast" Butler during the Civil War occupation.

St Louis Cathedral

Daily 7am–6.30pm. A postcard-perfect backdrop for the Andrew Jackson statue, St Louis Cathedral, commanding the square across Chartres Street, is the oldest continuously active cathedral in the United States, and the third church on this spot. Its construction in 1794 – the second church had been destroyed in the first of the city's

▼ ST LOUIS CATHEDRAL

two devastating fires, in 1788 – was funded, along with the Cabildo and the overhaul of the Presbytère, by the philanthropist Don Almonester; in 1850, while Almonester's daughter, the formidable Baroness Pontalba, was busy sprucing up the square around it, it was enlarged and remodeled by eminent architect J.N.B. de Pouilly. Dominated by three tall slate steeples, the dove-gray facade, which marries a Greek Revival symmetry with copious French arches, is oddly two-dimensional, like some elaborate stage prop for the lively street theater below.

Though the cathedral has always been central to the life of this very Catholic city – Andrew Jackson laid his sword on the altar in thanks for victory at the Battle of New Orleans; voodoo queen Marie Laveau (see p.88) was baptized and married here – the interior, a spruce assemblage of frescoes, sculpture, and stained glass, is modest. Behind the cathedral, on a patch of land that was the scene of numerous duels in the 1800s, is the pretty, iron-fenced St Anthony's Garden, where a huge marble statue of the Sacred Heart of Jesus casts an eerie shadow across the cathedral at night.

Pirate's Alley

Running between the cathedral and the Cabildo, this photogenic little street is supposedly where

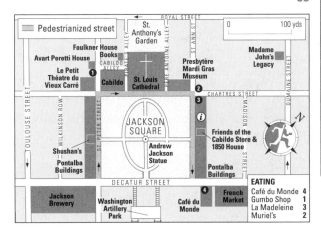

Andrew Jackson met local pirate Jean Lafitte and his band of buccaneers to ask for their aid in fighting the Battle of New Orleans in 1815. Highly unlikely, since the alley wasn't built until the 1830s – but it's a lovely spot nevertheless, lined with vibrantly colored town houses.

The Cabildo

Tues–Sun 9am–5pm; $5. On the upriver side of the cathedral, the Hispanic Cabildo was built as the Casa Capitular, seat of the Spanish colonial government. Today, it is home to an outstanding, people-oriented history museum. The building – which cuts an impressive dash with its columned arcade, fan windows, and fine wrought-iron balconies – is another legacy of the philanthropist

Don Almonester, who, after the original building burned in the fire of 1788, offered funds to remodel it in the grand style of the home country.

This museum ably picks its way through the complex tangle of cultures, classes, and races that binds together Louisiana's history. Crammed with well-captioned artifacts, it sets off with the Native Americans and winds up with the demise of Reconstruction – rather than attempting to see the whole place, it's best to concentrate on a few sections that particularly interest you.

In keeping with the city's fascination with matters morbid, there's a gloomy section devoted to disease, death, and mourning, while another displays the venom with which the White League-dominated Mardi Gras

The Louisiana State Museum

The Cabildo – along with the Presbytère, 1850 House, Old US Mint (p.62), and Madame John's Legacy (p.80) – is part of the Louisiana State Museum. Each site is open from Tuesday to Sunday from 9am to 5pm; buying a ticket to two or more gets you a discount of twenty percent, good for three consecutive days.

krewes (secret carnival clubs) resisted Reconstruction, barely masking their fury in racist, themed parades. Black history is well represented, with as much emphasis on the free people of color as on the city's role as the major slave-trading center of the South. Bills of sale show slaves priced for as much as $1350 each, while a worn-smooth auction block stands in front of an enlarged 1860 engraving depicting the markets held in the old St Louis Hotel (see p.78).

Other highlights include the bronze death mask of Napoleon, made and brought to New Orleans by the exiled emperor's doctor, and the room devoted to the Mississippi, at the back of the museum in the old Arsenal. Take a look at the Sala Capitular on the second floor, where, in 1803, the city of New Orleans – having been handed over just three weeks earlier from Spain to France – was sold by a cash-strapped Napoleon to the United States under the terms of the Louisiana Purchase.

It was here also that the historic 1892 Plessy vs Ferguson case, which legalized segregation throughout the South, was first argued.

The Presbytère Mardi Gras Museum

Tues–Sun 9am–5pm. $5. Forming a matching pair with the Cabildo, the Presbytère, on the downriver side of the cathedral, was designed in 1791 as a rectory. It was never used as such, however; the death of Don Almonester, its chief benefactor, put construction on hold, and it was not completed until 1813, when it went on to serve as a courthouse. Today it's an exceptionally good interactive Mardi Gras museum, which, by covering carnival from every conceivable angle, offers a penetrating look into the culture and history of the city.

Setting off by dealing with carnival's roots in Europe and Africa and illustrated with European carnival posters and vintage masks, much of

▼ THE CABILDO

the ground floor is concerned with official carnival. Here you can see close-up the extraordinary jewel-encrusted, ermine-trimmed costumes worn at private balls and in the formal parades. Some of the most dazzling exhibits date from the 1870s to 1890s, the golden age of carnival artistry, when old-line krewes Comus, Rex, Proteus, and Momus dominated the scene.

Unofficial carnival is covered in equal detail, with lots of good stuff on the Mardi Gras Indians

▲ MARDI GRAS MUSEUM

(see p.166), including a video of a Sunday-evening Indian practice, and fine examples of their flamboyant feather-and-bead "suits," painstakingly hand-sewn for a full year before being paraded on Mardi Gras morning. Another case holds costumes worn by lesser-known black carnival groups: the scary Skeletons, who originated in the 1930s, painting bones on tatty black suits and wearing massive *papier-mâché* skulls (their descendants, known as "bone gangs," occasionally parade with the Indians in Tremé), and the Baby Dolls – sassy groups of black women who, starting around 1912, would flounce through town on Mardi Gras day in big satin bonnets, short skirts, and bloomers. The section on gay Mardi Gras – a cornucopia of fantastic outfits – climaxes in a video of the notorious Bourbon Street awards, where gaggles of glamorous drag queens stagger under colossal get-ups as they compete for the prestigious best-costume prize.

The Pontalba Buildings

St Peter and St Ann sts bordering Jackson Square. A brace of imposing red-brick terraces elegantly framing the square, the Pontalba Buildings were commissioned in 1850 by the formidable Baroness Pontalba. Having been shot four times by her father-in-law in a violent row, lost two fingers, and divorced her husband, the baroness returned to her native New Orleans from Paris in 1849. Horrified to find her considerable real estate palling in comparison to the flourishing American sector across Canal Street, she sought to replace the shabby buildings around the Place d'Armes with elegant colonnaded structures resembling those she'd admired in France. The original architect, James Gallier Sr

▲ ARTIST IN JACKSON SQUARE

– who the baroness eventually sacked because of their endless squabbling – was responsible for many of the buildings' Greek Revival elements, but the large courtyards at the back, and the arrangement of commercial units on the ground floor with living spaces above, are typically Creole. These buildings were innovative in their use of mass-produced materials and, in particular, of cast iron – the iron was cast in New York, the red brick pressed in Baltimore, and the plate glass and slate roof tiles came from England. The stunning visual effect of the wide galleries and balconies,

their decorative curlicues centering on cartouches inscribed with the initials A&P – Almonester and Pontalba – sparked off a city-wide fad for lacy cast iron, which came to replace the plainer, hand-wrought iron fashioned locally by African slaves.

As the Quarter declined after the Civil War, the apartments lost their exclusivity, and by the end of the nineteenth century they had become tenements. In the 1920s, Sherwood Anderson, who along with William Faulkner, spearheaded the influx of writers into the Quarter in the 1920s, hosted important literary salons in his apartment here, and by the 1930s, restored by the WPA, they regained their former prestige. Today they are some of the city's most desirable places to live, with stores and restaurants.

1850 House

523 St Ann St. Tues–Sun 9am–5pm. $3. In 1850, when New Orleans was one of the largest cities in the US, riding on the wealth of its booming port, the Pontalba Buildings were the height of

▼ PONTALBA BUILDINGS

French Quarter architecture

While the French Quarter streets are as straight as a die, its architecture is a fabulous jumble. Little exists from before the city's two great fires of 1788 and 1794, after which the Spanish Governor ordained that all new buildings should be made of brick, plaster and stucco, with tiled roofs. Many of the vernacular buildings are one-story Creole cottages, and multistory Creole townhouses, both built about a foot off the ground above a closed ventilated area known as a "crawl space," and with a high gabled roof. Doors, indistinguishable from the outside from the shuttered ceiling-to-floor windows, open straight from the street into the living quarters. Planters from the West Indies built their houses on pillars, protecting them from waterlogging, and added porches – known as galleries – to shield against the sun and rain.

Under the Spanish, louvered shutters replaced heavier battened ones, and fine iron balconies were wrought by African craftsmen. Courtyards were designed as extra living areas, where residents cultivated tropical flowers, spices, and herbs to mask the odors from the street.

In the nineteenth century, Anglo-Americans tended to settle on the other side of Canal Street in what is now the CBD, but their influence was still felt in the Quarter, where a number of buildings were designed in simply elegant Federal or Greek Revival styles. The ornate cast iron, so associated with the Quarter, came in the 1840s, bought in bulk from the industrializing North. Inspired by the Pontalba Buildings on Jackson Square, a fad developed for filigree balconies and fences, curly brackets and fluted columns, which were added to old buildings and incorporated into new ones. In the late 1800s, shotgun houses emerged in force. Long, narrow clapboard structures composed of a single row of rooms opening onto each other, shotguns are most notable for the decorative wooden gingerbread details that early owners ordered from catalogs and stuck to the fronts.

fashion among the prosperous middle class. The cordoned-off rooms of the 1850 House, in the Lower Pontalba Buildings, re-create the tastes of a well-to-do Creole family from that era. Drawing attention to every piece of Rococo Revival furniture, Vieux Paris china, and fine crystal, but leaving little sense of how the family might have lived, this is the least interesting of the state museums to anyone but the most passionate fan of decorative arts.

Avart-Peretti House

632 St Peter St at Chartres. Built by J.N.B de Pouilly, the eminent local architect who also worked on St Louis Cathedral and Tremé's St Augustine's Church (see p.117), this 1842 townhouse was where Tennessee Williams wrote much of *A Streetcar Named Desire*. The Mississippi native, who said "If I can be said to have a home it is in the French Quarter, which has provided me with more material than any other part of the country," lived here during the winter of 1946/47, making final revisions to his manuscript *The Poker Night*. Working on his balcony to the accompaniment of "that rattletrap of a streetcar that bangs up one old street and down another" inspired him to rename and finish his work in progress, relocating it to New Orleans. Sadly, the streetcar itself, which ran through the Quarter to Desire Street in the Faubourg Marigny, stopped running in 1948.

▲ FAULKNER HOUSE BOOKS

Shops

Faulkner House Books

624 Pirate's Alley at Chartres ☎504/524-2940. Tucked into the lemon yellow building where the novelist lived in 1925 while writing his first novel, *Soldier's Pay*, this classy bookstore stocks titles by other Southern writers and many local-interest works, including first editions, rare books, and poetry. The owners are a great source of information on local literary events.

Friends of the Cabildo Store

523 St Ann St on Jackson Square ☎504/524-9118. Closed Mon. Especially good for local-interest books, this is also a great, central place to pick up New Orleans-related engravings, prints, CDs, jewelery, gifts, and cards.

Shushan's

536 St Peter St on Jackson Square ☎504/86-1188. This is by far the best place in the Quarter for men to kit themselves out in New Orleans style, with stylish, authentic guayabera shirts and a great selection of hats – from straw Panamas to green felt bowlers – at very good prices.

Cafés

Café du Monde

800 Decatur St at St Ann ☎504/581-2914. Daily 24hr. Despite the hype, the crowds, and the sugar-sticky tabletops, this old market coffeehouse is an undeniably atmospheric place to drink steaming café au lait, imbued with chicory, and snack on piping hot, sugary *beignets* for a couple of dollars – apart from orange juice and hot chocolate, they serve little else. Come early, when it's quiet, or join the night owls in the wee hours, when you can gaze at the starry sky from the covered patio.

▼ SHUSHAN'S

Restaurants

Gumbo Shop

630 St Peter St at Chartres
☎504/525-1486. A relaxed,
convivial spot for a quick lunch
or to fill up before a night out,
this touristy Creole restaurant
is housed in an eighteenth-
century building lined with
murals of old New Orleans.
Naturally the gumbo – seafood,
chicken and andouille, or
z'herbes – is the highlight; dark,
subtly flavored, and excellent
value ($4–7). Entrées are good,
too – try the crawfish étouffé
($12.95), or the succulent
grilled redfish smothered with
shrimp Creole ($14.95). The
combination dinners, three
courses plus side dish for
around $19, are a bargain.

La Madeleine

547 St Ann St at Chartres ☎504/568-
0073. The ambience is nothing
special, but it's the buttery
smells and fast counter service
that pull in the hungry artists
and footsore tourists into this
centrally located spot, part of
the national chain. Specialties
include crêpes, quiches, and pies,
as well as omelettes, pasta, and
fish; the boulangerie sells fresh
bread, pastries, and hot flaky
croissants to go.

Muriel's

801 Chartres St at St Ann ☎504/568-
1885, ⊛www.muriels.com. By far
the classiest dining option on
the square, with a number of
spacious, old-world rooms and
floor to ceiling windows that
they fling open on cool days.
The food, a mix of classic and
contemporary Creole, is tasty,
and, at lunchtime at least, not
too expensive – try the sampler
of jambalaya, crawfish étouffé,

▲ MURIEL'S

seafood gumbo, and red beans
and rice ($11 for two). Dinner
entrées (wood-grilled barbecue
shrimp, blackened lamb chops,
or eggplant ravioli) range from
$13–29; the three-course table
d'hôte, which starts at $22,
is good value. If you want
a sundowner and a snack,
the balcony (opens 3pm), a
wonderful vantage point over
Jackson Square, can't be beaten.

Performing arts

Petit Théâtre du Vieux Carré

616 St Peter St at Chartres ☎504/522-
2081, ⊛www.lepetittheatre.com.
The nation's longest-running
community theater, formed
in 1919 by the Drawing
Room Players, who first trod
the boards in private homes.
Today, it's a pretty setting for
middle-of-the-road musicals,
comedies, and drama, and an
atmospheric venue for the
annual Tennessee Williams
Literary Festival (see p.192).

French Quarter:
Decatur Street

When the French Quarter was laid out in 1721, Decatur Street (pronounced "deKAYter"), abutted the Mississippi. Today, the land that separates it from the water – four whole blocks of it at the Canal Street end – has all been dumped by the dramatically shifting river. A broad thoroughfare, noisy with traffic and lined with cheap-and-cheerful tourist shops, bars, and restaurants, Decatur becomes more countercultural as you head down-river, where, beyond the French Market, Lower Decatur's string of dive bars, funky restaurants, and thrift stores takes you into the hip Faubourg Marigny (see p.106).

▲ NHP VISITOR CENTER

Jean Lafitte National Historical Park Visitor Center

419 Decatur St at St Louis ☎504/589-2133. Daily 9am–5pm. Free. Something of an anomaly among Upper Decatur's brassy T-shirt shops and theme restaurants, the Jean Lafitte National Historical Park Visitor Center is tucked away behind a quiet courtyard. The park itself, comprised of natural and historic sites of interest scattered throughout southern Louisiana, includes the French Quarter, the Garden District, and the Chalmette Battlefield

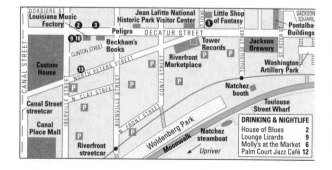

French Quarter: Decatur Street

(see p.101), and this visitor center is the starting point for excellent free walking tours (see p.191) as well as a rather good introduction to the Louisiana Delta and the city itself.

Beyond the illustrated panels and detailed timelines covering subjects as varied as the music, cuisine, religions, wildlife, and legends of this unique region, check out the listening stations, where Louisiana natives expound, in a variety of accents, on unique local words such as gumbo, *fais-do-do*, and, in the words of the song, *Iko Iko*. Touch-screen monitors show videos on jazz, brass bands, gospel, R&B, Cajun, and zydeco, with some rousing footage of Louis Armstrong, Mahalia Jackson, and Professor Longhair, among others. There's also a small bookshop, particularly strong on titles dealing with the city's early history.

The French Market

Spanning the riverside blocks that stretch downriver from Jackson Square to the US Mint, the French Market is said to stand on the site of a Choctaw trading area, and there was certainly active trade here, in one form or another, as early as the 1720s. Nineteenth-century visitors

▲ HOT SAUCE AT THE FRENCH MARKET

marveled at the exotic, chaotic jumble of Native Americans, Africans, Creoles, Sicilians, Chinese, Hindus, farmers, and fishermen, trading fragrant herbs, mysterious wild birds, and even alligators. The colonnaded arcades – much reworked and restored over the centuries – are more sanitized today, and much of the French Market is dominated by specialty stores teeming with tourists snapping up T-shirts, cookbooks, beads, masks, and pralines, while musicians play jazz outside crowded cafés.

PLACES French Quarter: Decatur Street

EATING

Café Angeli	8	Olivier's	10
Central Grocery	5	Rue de la Course	13
Fiorella's	11	Samurai Sushi	3
Johnny's Po-Boys	1	Tujague's	4
Maximo's	7		

The 24hr Farmers Market, which starts at the 1100 block of N Peters Street, is a wonderful source of fresh seasonal produce – depending on season, you'll find mountains of fresh pumpkins, sugarcane, Creole tomatoes, shrimp, sausages, and crabs sold around the clock, along with herbs, spices, coffee, hot sauce, and the like. On Wednesday, from 10am to 2pm, during the Crescent City Farmers Market, local farmers come in to sell organic produce from the backs of their trucks, with cooking demonstrations and lots of free tasters.

The 1200 block of N Peters Street is occupied by the daily flea market, a jumble of plants, jewelry, junk, and new and used clothes, with some interesting Latin American and African crafts among the trinkets. For a less touristy experience, it's just a short hop from here to the quirky thrift and rummage stores opposite on funky Lower Decatur Street.

▼ COCOMO JOE'S DRUM KIT, JAZZ MUSEUM

French Market Place

The innocuous alley that runs alongside the Farmers Market was known in the second half of the nineteenth century as Gallatin Street, the dingiest, deadliest block in New Orleans. Blind-drunk sailors and swaggering young blades would enter this cesspit of brothels, barrel houses, and dark gambling dens at their peril, many of them never to be seen again. Even policemen refused to set foot near the place. There's little to show for all this depravity today: just the market stalls on one side and the shabby back end of the Decatur shops on the other.

New Orleans Jazz National Historical Park Visitor Center

916 N Peters St at St Philip ☎504 /589-4841, ⊛www.nps/gov/jazz. Tues–Sat 9am–5pm. Free. Hidden away between the French Market and the river, the New Orleans Jazz National Historical Park Visitor Center is a must for any serious jazz fan. Though the park itself is still in development (plans include a performance and lecture space in Louis Armstrong Park), the free events staged here make it look very promising: master classes, concerts, movies, talks, walking tours, and workshops feature the very best local and visiting musicians and historians. Afterwards, check out the rare photographs, information sheets (including a selection of self-guided jazz walking tours), and the bookstore, which is, of course, packed with music titles and CDs.

Old US Mint/Jazz Museum

400 Esplanade Ave at Decatur. Tues–Sun 9am–5pm. $5 (20 percent discount with admission to any other museum in the State Museum group; see p.53). From 1838 to 1909

– with a break during the Civil War and Reconstruction – the Old US Mint churned out $300 million worth of currency, including, for a year or so, Confederate gold coins. First-floor exhibits tell the story of the building and of the backbreaking work entailed in nineteenth-century minting.

Most people, however, are here for the excellent Jazz Museum, which gives a good overview of, and background to, the music that New Orleans calls its own. Along with displays on most of the leading figures there's a fascinating historical timeline tracing the importance of disparate elements including minstrelsy, brass bands, the brothels of Storyville, and even opera to the art form. Among the wealth of photographs, sheet music, posters, advertising images and old letters (look out for the pencil-written fan mail from a 10-year-old Harry Connick Jr to pianist Armand Hug: "When I saw you play my eyes almost fell out!"), the highlights are the musical instruments, whose battered, well-worn contours are enough to bring tears to the eyes of any jazz buff. Among them is a cornet and bugle played by the young Louis Armstrong while learning his craft at the Waifs' Home; Kid Ory's trombone; Sidney Bechet's soprano sax; and a beautifully engraved horn played by Bix Beiderbecke. You'll find plenty of quirky humor alongside the reverence, from the "Lose Weight the Satchmo Way" brochure ("A laxative at least once a week is very nice!") to the customized tin-can drum kit made by street musician Cocomo Joe.

Despite the celebration, the genuine adulation and enthusiasm that has gone into putting this terrific collection together, however, small things, like a clumsily typed letter from jazz great Willie "Bunk" Johnson, bring a certain melancholy to the place. Poverty-stricken in his fading years, Johnson was reduced to writing to his old employer, begging him for a bicycle for his 68th birthday simply so he could get out to the shops.

The Mint also hosts temporary exhibits of decorative arts from the state museum collection: anything from oil paintings of nineteenth-century Creole nobility through Newcomb pottery – Louisiana's glorious contribution to the international arts and crafts movement – to folk art, and features a good little book and gift store.

Shops

Beckham's Bookshop

228 Decatur St at Bienville ☎ 504/522-9875. You could browse all day among the thousands of old

▼ BECKHAM'S BOOKSHOP

PLACES French Quarter: Decatur Street

editions, rare and out-of-print titles, and vintage magazines in this rambling, two-story bookstore.

Le Garage

1236 Decatur St at Barracks ☎504/522-6639. The biggest and the best of the rummage stores on this decadent stretch of Decatur: a warren of old uniforms, vintage Mardi Gras costumes, hats, suits, and dresses, along with furniture, junk, and books.

Jackson Brewery (JAX)

Decatur St between Toulouse and St Peter ☎504/566-7245. The least appealing of the downtown malls, filling a restored 1891 brewery with more than fifty brash stores. Among the ubiquitous pralines, hot sauces, and crawfish-emblazoned neckties, there's a Virgin Megastore, which has some good local stuff. The food court, despite its riverside terrace, is entirely missable.

▼ LOUISIANA MUSIC FACTORY

Little Shop of Fantasy

517 St Louis St at Decatur ☎504/529-4243. Closed Wed. Weird and wonderful designer masks, plus crucial festive accoutrements such as devil's horns, false eyelashes, tutus, strange hats, and velvet cloaks. They also do a nice line in offbeat gifts and books.

Louisiana Music Factory

210 Decatur St at Iberville ☎504/586-1094. A fantastic source of local music at good prices; nearly two full walls are lined with listening stations for jazz, R&B, gospel, Cajun, zydeco, and roots music. They also deal in vinyl, along with hard-to-find used music and books, plus posters, DVDs, and T-shirts. The expert staff organize frequent in-store performances.

Peligro

305 Decatur St at Bienville ☎504/581-1706. Treasure trove of contemporary Southern folk art and sculpture along with South American icons, tin boxes, and bottle-top saints. Prices range from very low to around $3000.

Rock and Roll Collectibles

1214 Decatur St at Gov Nicholls ☎504/561-5683. Particularly strong in rare vinyl, this shambolic old store sells the best in used blues, jazz, soul, and British imports. Prices can be steep ($80 for a rare Dr John LP, say, and as high as $600 in some cases) but are sometimes negotiable.

Tower Records

Riverfront Marketplace, 408 N Peters St ☎504/529-4411. Especially good for local sounds – the room dedicated to Louisiana

music has a wider choice than many of the specialist record stores – as well as rock, pop, and classical. They also stock videos, DVDs, and books – with the emphasis on alternative titles – and have a Ticketmaster stand (see p.197).

Cafés

Central Grocery
923 Decatur St at Dumaine ☎504/523-1620. Famed for its muffulettas (half for $5.50, whole for $9.75), this fragrant old Italian deli, open since 1906, offers a range of good picnic staples, with giant cheeses and salamis hanging from the ceiling and big tubs of olives marinating in herby oils. Most people take out – it's just a short hop across to the river – but there is some counter seating. No credit cards.

Rue de la Course
219 N Peters St at Iberville ☎504/523-0206. With its long, dimly lit room and air of perpetual gloom, this *Rue* is less appealing than the main Garden District branch (see p.141), but it's a useful location if you want to grab a well-made espresso drink or flavored tea to go. There are computer outlets at each table, and, unusually, a large smoking section.

Restaurants

Café Angeli
1141 Decatur St at Gov Nicholls ☎504/566-0077. Open daily till late; Fri & Sat 24hr. A hit with French Quarter night owls, hipsters, and barflies, this big, open, dimly lit room is virtually an extension of the Lower Decatur scene outside. Picture windows

▲ ARTIST OUTSIDE FIORELLA'S

allow diners to see and be seen, while cult movies flicker across the wall above the bar. Its late hours are welcome, and the Mediterranean salads, sandwiches, fresh pizzas, and pasta are just the thing after a wild night out.

Fiorella's
45 French Market Place/1136 Decatur St at Gov Nicholls ☎504/528-9566. A French Quarter classic, this down-home French Market diner has long been a local favorite for its cheap blue-plate specials ($6.50 for red beans and rice, fried catfish, or meatloaf), crawfish dishes, and simply amazing fried chicken ($6.50–8.25 with sides and potatoes).

Johnny's Po-Boys
511 St Louis St at Decatur ☎504/524-8129. This no-frills, checked-tablecloth joint is heaving at lunchtime with

▲ JOHNNY'S PO-BOYS

local workers and repeat-visit tourists. It's famed for its massive po-boys, of course, made to order – the mind-boggling choice of fillings includes pork chop, French fries, chicken Parmesan, boudin, oysters, roast beef, and catfish – but they also serve good breakfasts and plate lunches ($6–11). Prepare to wait at lunchtime, or call for deliveries. No credit cards.

Maximo's

1117 Decatur St at Ursulines ☎504/586-8883. Northern Italian food in a slick urban bistro, with counter seating, booths, and moody jazz photos. It's especially buzzy at weekends, when people pile in to eat late. You can't go wrong with the pasta, especially penne crawfish diablo in a zippy cream sauce, and the veal is great, be it cooked with garlic, lemon and wine, or pan-roasted with herbs. There's zabaglione to finish and fifty good Italian wines (from a list of around 300), many served by the glass.

Olivier's

204 Decatur St at Iberville ☎504/525-7734. Delicious black Creole food, served in elegant

surroundings in a charming old building. The menu at this welcoming, family-owned spot describes how each dish is cooked according to the recipe of a different family member. To start, they offer four gumbos – the Creole variety is fantastic, packed with sausage and shrimp – entrées include poulet au fromage, baked with five cheeses and served with shrimp, and Creole rabbit with oyster stuffing doused in a dark, herby sauce. They also do an expert crawfish étouffé, finely flavored and not as gloopy as it sometimes can be, and a killer butter-and-rum bread pudding.

Samurai Sushi

239 Decatur St at Bienville ☎504/525-9595. Closed lunch Sat & Sun. The only sushi bar in the Quarter, this sleek, minimal place offers good rolls and nigiri from $3.50, along with sushi and sashimi plates (around $20), baked wasabi mussels, udon noodle soups, teriyaki, and a plate of tasty monkfish livers served with ponzu sauce. The lunch specials are a good deal, especially the sushi combo ($9.75).

Tujague's

823 Decatur St at Madison ☎504/525-8676. Eating in this classic New Orleans dining room has changed little since the 1850s, when butchers, dockers, and French Market traders dined on *Tujague's* famed seven-course Creole feasts – the table d'hôte starts with shrimp rémoulade, soup, and a meltingly tender boiled brisket with Creole sauce, goes on to offer a choice of three classic entrées, and closes with bread pudding and coffee.

Depending on your entrée, you'll pay about $30 – but it's not really done to ask the price in advance. There's also a beautiful old stand-up bar that's particularly good fun on Sunday, when regulars gather to catch up and gossip, and from which you can order a boiled brisket po-boy or a scrumptious chicken Bonne Femme (fried with heaps of garlic and parsley).

Bars

Molly's at the Market

1107 Decatur St at Ursulines ☎504/525-5169. Once famed for being a genuine local Irish bar, haunt of politicos and media stars, *Molly's* now pulls in a happy mix of locals, rowdy tourists, service industry workers and grungy street punks. It's a very New Orleans kind of place, stubbornly remaining open during hurricane alerts, and organizing street parades for Mardi Gras, St Patrick's Day, and Halloween. There's Guinness on tap and paninis, salads, burgers, and pasta from the kitchen at the back.

Live music and clubs

House of Blues

225 Decatur St at Iberville ☎504/529-BLUE, ⊛www.hob.com. Slick venue, part of the national chain, with Southern folk-art-themed decor. While the high prices and highly un-New Orleans attitude (bouncers, wrist tags) can be off-putting, they book the best in everything from blues, funk, reggae, and zydeco to rap, hip-hop, and rock, with regular appearances from big names like Bob Dylan, Ray Charles, Johnny Cash, and Lee "Scratch" Perry. There's a gospel brunch on Sunday (9.30am, 11.45am & 2pm; call to reserve) and regular DJ dance nights. Local bands also play at the smaller Parish Room upstairs.

Lounge Lizards

200 Decatur St at Iberville ☎504/598-1500. With its comfy, fusty velvet sofa, eclectic jukebox, and laid-back, hip staff, this

▼ HOUSE OF BLUES

PLACES French Quarter: Decatur Street

▲ PALM COURT JAZZ CAFÉ

very dark bar might be more at home somewhere on alternative Lower Decatur than up here opposite the *House of Blues*. It's a welcoming place, attracting a friendly, alternative crowd of regulars as well as a few stray tourists. Nightly live music includes Delta blues, R&B, and roots bands; Wednesday heralds Twisted Karaoke, when worse-for-wear wannabes can belt out a selection of rock/punk tracks along with a live band.

Palm Court Jazz Café

1204 Decatur St at Gov Nicholls ☎504/525-0200, ⊛www .palmcourtcafe.com. Closed Mon & Tues. Top-notch trad jazz played in convivial supper-club surroundings. It's a classically New Orleans dining room, lined with jazz photos – they also sell collector's items and records. Reservations are recommended for dinner, which is nothing special and rather pricey; you might do better simply to sit at the bar. Shows 8pm; cover $5.

French Quarter:
Chartres Street

Bisected by Jackson Square, **Chartres Street** (pronounced "Charders") is quieter and far less commercial than Decatur, its appealing mix of bars, patisseries, and offbeat shops geared as much to locals as to tourists. It was here that the great fire of Good Friday 1788 broke out, after a candle in a small household shrine set light to a curtain; all told, 856 buildings, including St Louis Cathedral (see p.52), were destroyed in its wake.

The Napoleon House

500 Chartres St at St Louis. Now a hugely atmospheric bar and restaurant, the Napoleon House is in fact made up of two houses. The original, 1797 building is a two-story structure on St Louis; the elegant three-story building on Chartres was added in 1814. With its weatherbeaten stucco walls, heavy wooden shutters, and cupola, it's one of the loveliest buildings in the Quarter, and even more so inside. The main house was built for Mayor Nicholas Girod, who, so the story goes, volunteered to host the exiled French emperor. Sometimes the story goes even further, claiming that, with the help of pirates Jean Lafitte and Dominique You, Girod sent a boat to rescue Napoleon from the island of St Helena – unaware that he had died three days before it set sail.

Historical Pharmacy Museum

514 Chartres St at St Louis. Tues–Sun 10am–5pm. $5. Housed in an 1820s apothecary – in a Creole-American townhouse designed by J.N.B. de Pouilly, who also remodeled St Louis Cathedral – this quirky museum offers fascinating insights into the history of medicine. Huge rosewood cabinets are filled with ancient glass jars crammed with herbs, froufrou china containers advertising Creole miracle cures, old medical books and ledgers, and terrifying

▼ THE NAPOLEON HOUSE

surgical implements. Look out for the 1850s trephination drill, a savage saw-toothed corkscrew that was bored into the skull in the belief that it might cure a headache, and the scarefier, a nineteenth-century blood-letting apparatus with twelve razor-sharp blades. Perhaps worst of all is the present-day leech mobile home, a jar filled with fat, lurking leeches, just waiting to suck on the tissue of cosmetic or reconstructive surgery patients. There's lots of gruesome detail here on the epidemics that ravaged the city in the nineteenth century, particularly yellow fever, or "black vomit," for which the purging, bleeding, and blistering tried by the doctors did nothing to prevent it felling one tenth of the population in one year alone.

A voodoo cabinet reveals the *gris-gris* – charms, or spells, sold under the counter in many nineteenth-century New Orleans pharmacies – to have been nothing more mysterious than essential oils. Other voodoo remedies – for syphilis, say, or mastitis (mouldy bread soaked in milk, and sheep-manure tea, respectively) were less pleasant.

Upstairs, along with an intriguing exhibition on the history of spectacles and eyepieces, there's a display on women's medicine, with jars of quack remedies (complete with details of their dismal side effects) and barbaric gynecological speculums.

▼ VOODOO POTIONS, HISTORICAL PHARMACY MUSEUM

The Beauregard-Keyes House

1113 Chartres St at Ursulines.
Tours hourly Mon–Sat 10am–3pm.
$5. This raised 1826 Creole
cottage owes the first part of its
name to Confederate General
Pierre Beauregard, who rented
a room here for a couple of
years during Reconstruction.
Beauregard ordered the first
shot of the Civil War at Fort
Sumter and remained a hero
in the South long after the
war was lost. In the 1940s, the
house was bought by popular
novelist Frances Parkinson
Keyes, who wrote many of her
New Orleans-based titles here.
Tour guides tend to skim over
the years in between, when the
French Quarter had declined
into a slum, populated mostly
by the poor Italians who came
to the city
in the 1890s.
Today, at pains
to present itself
as an eminently
genteel place, the
house works best
as a museum
of decorative
arts, showcasing
a wide range
of fine old
furniture, from
Beauregard's
rosewood
armoires to
Keyes' New
England-made
pieces.

The Old Ursuline Convent

1114 Chartres St at Ursulines. Tours
Tues–Fri 10am, 11am, 1pm, 2pm &
3pm, Sat & Sun 11.15am, 1pm &
2pm. $5. Built between 1745 and
1750, the tranquil Old Ursuline
Convent is the only intact
French Colonial structure in
the city, and quite possibly the
oldest building in the Mississippi
Valley. The Ursuline nuns arrived
in New Orleans from France
in 1727, just ten years after the
city was established, to nurse the
soldiers of the early colony. In
1729 they built an orphanage
for the children of colonists
killed in the Indian rebellion at
Fort Rosalie in Mississippi; they
also taught (segregated) classes
for young Creole, African, and
Native American girls. Since
1824, when the nuns moved to a

▼ ST MARY'S CHAPEL

new site, the imposing, dove-gray building – typically French-Canadian, with its tall casement windows and steeply pitched roof – has served variously as a school, the seat of the state legislature, and the archbishopric. Inside, the mishmash of religious paraphernalia includes brightly colored bishops' slippers (red for martyrdom, green for hope) and the heavy wooden "Doorway to Heaven," a table on which bishops lay in state in St Louis Cathedral.

In the 1846 St Mary's Chapel next door, a Baroque marble altar displays an overwrought scene of the Revelation and the Virgin Mary, who pops up again on the stained-glass windows; to the right of the altar, she's shown above a foggy view of the Battle of New Orleans.

Shops

The Centuries

408 Chartres St at Conti ☎504/568-9491. The laid-back staff here is happy to let you browse antique prints and maps, engravings, and etchings. Categories of note include local interest, architecture, countries, fashion, and literature.

A Gallery for Fine Photography

241 Chartres St at Bienville ☎504/568-1313. Closed Sun & Mon. Superb antique and classic photographs to look at or to buy. Many prices reach four figures, and rare platinum prints can go for as much as $12,500. Works date from 1839 and include pictures by Edward S. Curtis, WeeGee, Diane Arbus, Helmut Newton, and David Bailey. Look out for Walker Evans' photos of the 1930s French Quarter, a host of jazz portraits, and Clarence White's ghostly double-exposed images. The books section includes rare nineteenth-century titles.

Lucullus

610 Chartres St at Wilkinson Row ☎504/528-9620. Sept–May closed Sun, June–Aug closed Mon. Named for the Roman general who held notoriously lavish banquets, this is a wonderful place for dining-related antiques – coffee pots, linens, earthenware jars, Art Deco china – dating from the 1600s onwards.

Magic Bus

527 Conti St at Chartres ☎504/522-0530. It may not have as varied a choice as some of the others, but this old record store does offer bargains, especially on local jazz and blues cassettes. Also features new, used, and rare CDs and vinyl.

▼ MAGIC BUS

▲ LA MARQUISE

Rouge Beauty

539 Dumaine St at Chartres
℡504/525-8686. Not your average
cosmetics and accessories store:
come here for all things stylish,
vampish, cute, and sparkly in
most price ranges.

Trashy Diva

829 Chartres St at Madison
℡504/581-4555. Exquisite, top-
of-the-range period clothes;
beautiful 1940s suits, 1930s
evening wear, corsages, nippy
little hats, costume jewelry, and
a wide range of sexy antique
corsets. Their own line of
vintage-look chiffon dresses and
satin dresses is as exquisite and
expensive as the real thing.

Cafés

La Marquise

625 Chartres St at Wilkinson Row
℡504/524-0420. With its tempting
French pastries, croissants, and
quiches, this neighborhood

patisserie, sister shop to the
Croissant d'Or (see p.83), is a
good little spot for breakfast.
The unpretentious French
Quarter vibe and local clientele
make it a pleasant place to
linger, either in the cozy rose-
pink interior or in the shady
courtyard. No credit cards.

Napoleon House

500 Chartres St at St Louis ℡504/524-
9752. This fabulous old bar is
one of the city's best lunch
stops. Everyone comes here
for the muffulettas, which they
heat up to melt the cheese
and mellow the flavors, but it's
worth branching out to try their
other Mediterranean sandwiches
(the Franco, say, packed with
herby mushroom salad, spinach,
and mozzarella), gumbos,
and salads (the Greek comes
with baby spinach, roasted
red peppers, and warm grilled
flatbread). There's also a terrific
full-service bistro on site; see
Girod's, below.

▲ GIROD'S BISTRO

Restaurants

Bacco

310 Chartres St at Bienville, in the
W Hotel ☏504/522-2426. This
gorgeous, unstuffy nouvelle
Italian – all Venetian chandeliers,
Gothic-style iron arches, and
ivory-colored booths scrawled
with Italian love proclamations
– is less expensive than you
might expect, especially at
lunch, when you can get two
courses for around $18, along
with astonishingly tangy 10¢
martinis. Dinner can set you
back, however, especially if you
order foie gras pizza ($18), and
the tasty home-made pasta
can be pricey. Good appetizers
include roasted garlic soup, rich
with Romano cheese, while for
an entrée you could try wood-
oven-roasted Gulf shrimp with
greens, penne, and feta dressing.
The tiramisu is great, too.

Girod's Bistro

500 Chartres St at St Louis
☏504/522-4152, ⊛www
.napoleonhouse.com. Closed Sun
& Mon. Wonderful, romantic
restaurant, linked to the
Napoleon House and hidden
away beside its pretty courtyard.
The bistro is all cracked plaster,
candlelight, and paintings
– the perfect setting to linger
over robust, creative Creole
food with Mediterranean and
Caribbean accents. Appetizers
($6–9) are a meal in themselves:
try the shellfish cake in Creole
mustard reduction. Of the
entrées ($13–25), most of
which come with unusual,
flavorful sauces, sure-fire
winners include the Louisiana
shellfish with angel hair pasta
and wild mushrooms.

K-Paul's Louisiana Kitchen

416 Chartres St at Conti ☏504/524-
7394, ⊛www.kpauls.com. Closed
lunch Tues–Thurs. Renowned,
rustic-smart restaurant serving
the "blackened" cuisine,
slathered in butter and spices,
introduced to the nation by
Cajun chef Paul Prudhomme
in the 1980s. If you like your
food hot and heavy you'll love
it here; highlights among dinner
entrées (around $30) include
bronzed swordfish with "Hot
Fanny" sauce – roasted pecans,
jalapeños, veal glaze, and garlic
butter. Gumbos are rich: try the
wild turkey and andouille. Most
diners are tourists who wait for
ages for a table (reservations
are accepted only for the more
formal upstairs room); come for
lunch, when lines are shorter,
prices far lower, and there's time
to walk it all off.

▲ K-PAUL'S

rice, jambalaya, barbecue ribs, crawfish pie, shrimp Creole, Louisiana yams, vegetable and bread pudding (which, covered with a hot praline sauce, you should order for dessert anyway). The cheaper lunch menu (11am–4pm) includes po-boys and big plates of red beans and rice with fried chicken.

Bars

Napoleon House

500 Chartres St at St Louis ☎504/524-9752, ⊛www.napoleonhouse.com. Exuding a classic, relaxed New Orleans elegance, the *Napoleon House* is quite simply one of the best bars in the United States. The shadowy interior is romantic in the extreme, its crumbling walls lined with age-blackened oil paintings and the old, well-stocked wooden bar dominated by a marble bust of the frowning emperor. The customers, an interesting mix of tourists and regulars, dally for hours, either indoors, where chatter mingles with classical music on the CD player, or in

Rita's

945 Chartres St at St Philip ☎504/525-7543. Cozy black Creole restaurant in an unpretentious dining room lined with news clippings and photos. The food is substantial, tasty, and good value: for dinner, try the blow-out "Taste of New Orleans" ($16) – gumbo, red beans and

▼ NAPOLEON HOUSE COURTYARD

the gorgeous courtyard, fringed with lush plants.

Live music

One-Eyed Jack's

615 Toulouse St at Chartres ☎504/569-8361. Creative, hip bar/club that successfully throws together an offbeat mix of music and styles. Loosely conceived as a decadent cabaret lounge in old Bourbon Street style, *Jack's* is slightly dark and a little daring, but it's a friendly place for all that, and never takes itself too seriously. Live shows include burlesque, traditional jazz, swing, R&B, and indie. Cover varies.

▲ BURLESQUE, ONE EYED JACK'S

French Quarter: Royal Street

Elegant **Royal Street** was the main commercial thoroughfare of the Creole city, inhabited by the wealthiest sugar planters and lined with the finest shops. Despite being one of the most touristed routes through the Quarter, it's still a dignified old place, lined with landmark buildings, antique stores, and small, chic art galleries. Its fabulous cast-iron balconies create a stunning streetscape familiar from countless movies, coffeetable books, and postcards.

Exchange Alley

A pedestrianized lane running parallel to Royal Street between Canal and Conti, Exchange Alley was originally intended to lead all the way to the Cabildo. It never got further than the St Louis Hotel, however – making a convenient conduit from the American sector straight into the hotel's slave exchange.

In the 1800s this was the "street of the fencing masters," inhabited almost exclusively by skilled teachers who trained young men in the art of dueling. Duels, or *affaires d'honneur*, had long been part of the fabric of the French and Spanish colony, fought with rapiers by proud young Creoles and settled at "first blood"; however, as the city Americanized and rifles became the weapons of choice, duels became contests to the death.

Bienville and Iberville streets

Exchange Alley cuts across Bienville and Iberville streets, which run parallel to Canal. The Vieux Carré Commission, founded in the 1930s with the mandate to preserve the "quaint and distinctive character" of the French Quarter (or Vieux Carré – "old square"), has no responsibility for these two streets, and despite the occasional new development, the sleazy, pre-preservation Quarter is revealed in all its dingy glory in the shabby buildings and lots, 1950s neon, and dim, dank girlie bars.

▼ ROYAL STREET BALCONIES

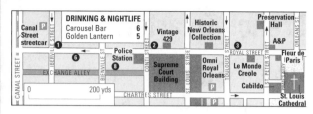

The Supreme Court Building

In 1910, when the Quarter was at its most run-down and the Vieux Carré Commission barely dreamed of, an entire block, bounded by Royal, St Louis, Chartres, and Conti, was demolished to make way for a colossal new courthouse. Abandoned in the 1950s in favor of more modern premises in the Central Business District, the Beaux Arts behemoth was finally restored in 2004 to house the Louisiana Supreme Court.

Though the sheer scale of the place makes it an incongruous sight in the narrow streets of the Quarter, its glossy, veined marble facade, gleaming behind huge green palms, makes it an undeniably handsome one.

Omni Royal Orleans Hotel

At the corner of Royal and St Louis, the swanky *Omni Royal Orleans Hotel* stands on the site of the famed *St Louis Hotel*, designed in 1838 by J.N.B. de Pouilly. With its copper dome, colossal spiral staircase, and opulent frescoes, the St Louis was at the heart of Creole high society, hosting the grandest balls, and, in its columned, marble rotunda, holding the city's largest slave exchange. To encourage traders to stay the full three hours between noon and 3pm, when auctioneering took place, management offered them a free lunch at the bar – a canny promotion that spread like wildfire through taverns around the nation until the onset of Prohibition.

During the city's shambolic Reconstruction period, it housed the State Capitol, but was abandoned in 1898 and left to decay for years. A hurricane blasted off the roof in 1915, and the wrecked building was finally demolished a year later, to

▼ SUPREME COURT BUILDING

EATING	
Brennan's	2
CC's Community	
Coffeehouse	4
Court of Two Sisters	3
Croissant d'Or	9
Lulu's	8
Mona Lisa	7
Mr B's Bistro	1

be replaced in 1960 with the swanky *Omni Royal*. At the back of the hotel, on Chartres Street, you can still make out the shadow of the word "exchange," painted on blocks of stone taken from the original building.

Historic New Orleans Collection

533 Royal St at Toulouse. Tues–Sat 10am–4.30pm; tours 10am, 11am, 2pm & 3pm. $4. In 1938, wealthy plantation owners General Kemper and Mrs Leila Williams bought and restored the 1792 Merieult House – one of the few survivors of the 1794 fire – along with a neighboring structure around the corner on Toulouse Street. Entry to the excellent temporary history exhibitions (on subjects ranging from Mardi Gras to maps) in the street-front room of the Merieult House is free, but to see the best of the collection you'll need to take a guided tour, which might cover the ten galleries upstairs, or the Williams House on Toulouse.

The extensive main collection is a fascinating treasure-trove of old maps, drawings, architectural

▼ HISTORIC NEW ORLEANS COLLECTION

plans, documents relating to the Louisiana Purchase, furniture, and paintings. Highlights include the only known portrait painted from life of the French-Canadian explorer Sieur de Bienville, first governor of the colony of Louisiana and, in 1717, founder of the city of Nouvelle Orléans, and two revealing portraits of Andrew Jackson – furrow-browed and quizzical in 1819, and far more world-weary 21 years later, after his stint as the seventh US president. Look out, too, for the 1720 engraving that portrays the colony as a land of milk and honey peopled with beaming natives – an early publicity poster put out by John Law's Company of the West to attract settlers from Europe to what was, in reality, an unprepossessing, disease-ravaged swamp.

For anyone interested in design and decorative arts, the 1889 Williams House, 718 Toulouse St (reached via Merieult House), is a must. Objects include a stool fashioned out of a column from a demolished plantation, lamps made from samovars and antique Chinese burial art, and a host of antique maps.

Madame John's Legacy

628 Dumaine St at Royal. Tues–Sun 9am–5pm. $3 (20 percent discount with admission to any other museum in the State Museum group; see p.53). A rare example of the French Quarter's early, West Indies-style architecture, Madame John's Legacy was rebuilt after the fire of 1788 as an exact replica of the 1730 house that had previously stood on the site. It was constructed using the *briquette entre poteaux* technique, in which soft red brick is set between steadying, hand-hewn cypress beams, and raised off the ground on stucco-covered brick pillars. The deep wraparound gallery provided extra living space, cooler and airier than the indoor rooms.

Though today it stands flush with the street, in the days of the French colony it would have been surrounded by far more land. On the ground floor, an illuminating exhibition details the house's various changes in fortune; go through the courtyard to the upper level to see a superb museum of affecting Southern folk art.

▼ ROYAL STREET ANTIQUE STORE

There never was an actual Madame John – the name was given to the house by the wildly popular nineteenth-century author George Washington Cable in his tragic short story "'Tite Poulette," and it simply stuck, attracting hundreds of book-loving tourists to the city and spawning a nice line in Madame John souvenirs.

Gallier House

1132 Royal St at Ursulines. Tours hourly on the half-hour Mon–Sat 10.30am–3.30pm. $6, $10 with the Hermann-Grima House, see p.86. The handsome 1857 Gallier House – reputedly Anne Rice's inspiration for Louis and Lestat's dwelling in her novel *Interview with the Vampire* – was built for his family by James Gallier Jr, a leading architect like his father before him. Though it's in many ways a typical Creole structure, with a large carriageway leading to a courtyard, Gallier also incorporated a number of American elements, such as the enclosed hall and indoor bathroom. Innovations include a cooling system and a flushing toilet, while the filigree cast-iron galleries would have been the last word in chic.

Tours offer a welcome focus on social history. The place is set up to re-create the cluttered style of the antebellum era, when the citywide fashion for fancy decoration had to be balanced with the practicalities of living in a swampy climate: fine oil paintings and hand-carved closets stand tilted away from the walls, to avoid being blighted by mildew. Though city slaves were regarded as being better off than field laborers, who did the back-breaking work of the plantations, life was by no means easy, as a quick wander around the slave quarters reveals. These small rooms were minimally furnished with old or broken furniture from the main house, and because slave skins were thought to be "tough," were free of mosquito netting.

The LaLaurie Home

1140 Royal St at Gov Nicholls. Not open to the public. The French Empire LaLaurie Home is the most famous haunted house in New Orleans. In the nineteenth century this gloomy gray and black pile, now an apartment block, belonged to the LaLauries, a doctor and his socialite wife Delphine, who, although seen wielding a whip as she chased a slave girl through the house to the roof, was merely fined when the child fell to her death. Whispers about the couple's cruelty were horribly verified when neighbors rushed in after a fire in 1834 – believed to have been started intentionally by the shackled cook – to find seven emaciated slaves locked in the attic. The next day the pair escaped the baying mob outside their home and fled to France. Since then, many claim to have heard ghostly moans from the building at night; some say they have seen a girl stumble across the balcony.

During Reconstruction the building housed a desegregated girls' school, a hopeful venture that ended in December 1874 when the White League militia, a group of ex-Confederates committed to stamping out what they called the "Africanization" of their city, stormed in and evicted by force any of the pupils they believed to have African blood.

▲ FIFI MAHONY'S

Shops

A&P

701 Royal St at St Peter ☎504/523-1353. Open 24hr. The smallest *A&P* in the world is the largest supermarket in the Quarter, and always bustling: you'll rub shoulders with horn players and living statues, tourists, and bus boys all "making groceries," as shopping for food is known in these parts. There's a deli counter at the back, and a good selection of fresh fruit and salad vegetables.

Bergen Galleries

730 Royal St at Père Antoine Alley ☎504/523-7882. Prints and posters, including local artists Michalopoulos (who does vivid, dreamlike streetscapes) and Rodrigue (whose little blue dog pops up everywhere), along with Vargas and Erté, etchings, and the best Jazz Fest and Mardi Gras posters.

Fifi Mahony's

934 Royal St at St Philip ☎504/525-4343. Fabulous wig store, staffed by gorgeous boys and girls with neon hair and glittering eyelids. You can try the hairpieces at a big, lightbulb-edged mirror, or rifle through all manner of nail polish, hair mascara, and eye jewels.

Fleur de Paris

712 Royal St at Pirate's Alley ☎504/525-1900. Renowned for its ultra-glamorous window displays, Fleur de Paris specializes in flamboyant custom-made hats, uptown evening wear, and cocktail dresses – prices are high, but then, this place is practically a work of art.

Grace Note

900 Royal St at Dumaine ☎504/522-1513. Offbeat store selling fabulous hats, vintage and designer women's clothes, jewelry, and gloves – all very New Orleans, with lots of velvets, satins, embroidery, and fringing. Check out the 1930s-style chiffon dresses: perfect for debauchery on a wrought-iron balcony.

Historic New Orleans Collection

533 Royal St at St Louis ☎504/523-4662. Closed Sun & Mon. Terrific, reasonably priced museum store with a great collection of old maps and prints on subjects including New Orleans, the Civil War, Napoleon, and Audubon's "botanicals." Also postcards (early city plans, paintings of the Quarter in the 1930s, old photos, etc), and shelves of new and used books.

Hové Parfumeur

824 Royal St at St Ann ☎504/525-7827. Closed Sun. There's a distinctly old-world ambience

▲ HOVÉ PARFUMEUR

at this elegant, rose-pink and black parfumier, which has been around since the 1930s. Best seller is the Tea Olive, made from the sweet olive blossom, common in New Orleans gardens; sniff out too the Magnolia, Carnaval, and musky Rue Royale.

Gerald D. Katz

505 Royal St at St Louis ☎504/524-5050. One of Royal Street's classic antique stores, a grand old place with the nation's largest hoard of nineteenth-century jewelry, plus china and oil paintings.

Le Monde Creole

624 Royal St at Toulouse ☎504/568-1801. Superb, eclectic little store set back from the street in a ravishing courtyard. Run by the people who lead the excellent city and plantation tours (p.191), it specializes in shabby-chic objets d'art and furnishings, postcards, prints, CDs, and videos, all related to the Creoles. Also a great selection of books

on Storyville, music, slave history, black folk tales, and more.

Verti Marte

1201 Royal St at Gov Nicholls ☎504/525-4767. Open 24hr. Decrepit corner grocery with an astonishingly good hot-food take-out counter: pick up mountains of baked chicken, fried oysters, barbecue ribs, stuffed eggplant, macaroni, dirty rice, and gumbo for ridiculously low prices.

Vintage 429

429 Royal St at St Louis ☎504/529-2288. Scores of autographed first editions, rare vinyl and photos, from local boy Kermit Ruffins through Elvis to Greta Garbo (whose autographed picture will set you back $4000) and the elusive J.D. Salinger. Cheaper stuff includes 1950s cocktail sets, lunchboxes, cigarette cases, and concert posters.

Cafés

CC's Community Coffeehouse

941 Royal St at St Philip ☎504/581-6996. Locals linger for hours at the counter or in the plump leather armchairs, chatting or people-watching through the open French windows. The brews are good and strong – try the Mochasippi, a creamy iced espresso with a choice of flavors. Also smoothies, quiches, pastries, and muffins. No smoking.

Croissant d'Or

617 Ursulines St at Royal ☎504/524-4663. Peaceful, old-fashioned little café in a converted ice-cream parlor. Here you'll get the best French pastries and stuffed croissants this side of Paris, plus quiches, salads, and steaming

▲ CROISSANT D'OR

café au lait. There's a courtyard, but inside, with its marble floor, tiled walls, stained glass, and iron chairs, is usually filled with locals reading, writing, and chatting. No smoking indoors and $10 minimum for credit cards.

Restaurants

Brennan's

417 Royal St at Conti ☎504/525-9711, ⊛www.brennansneworleans.com.
Historic Creole restaurant, the first in the city's Brennan empire, with a dozen dining rooms and a tropical courtyard. It's famed for its long, luxurious breakfasts (served until 2.30pm) – choose from more than twenty poached-egg dishes, hair-of-the-dog cocktails, grillades and grits, and the like; though locals balk at spending $50 on eggs, tourists can't get enough of the place. Dinner proves better value, with four-course meals for $38.50: the long menu includes turtle and oyster soups, shrimp *sardou* (with

an artichoke, spinach, and hollandaise sauce), the definitive Bananas Foster, and wonderful café brulot, while the winelist runs to 65 pages. Dress up and reserve.

Court of Two Sisters

613 Royal St between St Peter and Toulouse ☎504/522-7261, ⊛www .courtoftwosisters.com.
New Orleans' only daily jazz brunch, where a Dixieland trio plays 45-minute sets in a huge, wisteria-draped brick courtyard. Gorge on a huge choice of local specialties including spicy oysters, turtle soup, sweet potato with andouille, Bananas Foster, and bread pudding, along with mounds of boiled seafood. It's not gourmet, but tasty and reasonably priced at $25. Reserve.

Lulu's

307 Exchange Alley at Bienville ☎504/525-2600. Closed Sun & Mon.
This tiny place, relaxed, quiet and with outdoor seating, has caused a citywide stir for its simple, good soups, salads, and sandwiches. It may not be very New Orleans, but a citrus, beet, and fennel salad with a jar of home-made lemonade will come as a welcome relief if you've been overdoing it with the rich sauces and lethal cocktails.

Mona Lisa

1212 Royal St at Barracks ☎504/522-6746. Candlelit at night, with brick walls, cobblestone floors, and wine coolers made from battered olive-oil cans, this funky, friendly place is a favorite with Quarterites. You can get pasta, sandwiches, and salads,

▲ COURT OF TWO SISTERS JAZZ BRUNCH

but the pizzas are the best thing here; try the Mediterranean, with spinach, feta, garlic, olives, and sun-dried tomatoes. A 12in ($11–15) is more than enough for two. Choose from the wine list, or BYOB.

Mr B's Bistro

201 Royal St at Iberville ☎504/523-2078. Another Brennan winner: a casually chic European-style bistro with dark-wood booths, lots of etched glass, a piano player, relaxed, chatty buzz, and spectacular food. The star-studded contemporary Creole menu boasts the city's finest garlic chicken, served in a satiny reduction, and delectable barbecue shrimp in a sloppy, rich, buttery sauce – you'll need the bib they tie around your neck. It can get pricey, so if you're on a budget, try it for lunch. They always accept walk-ins.

Bars

Carousel Bar

Hotel Monteleone, 214 Royal St at Iberville ☎504/523-3341. Kitted out like a fairground carousel, with the stools set on a revolving floor, the bar at this hotel lounge takes fifteen minutes to do one full rotation. Drinks

are a little pricey, but you get free snacks, and it's a fun stop on a French Quarter bar crawl. If you're feeling dizzy you can settle at stationary booths illuminated by a trompe l'oeil starlit sky, but that's missing the point somewhat. Live jazz piano Wed–Sat from 9pm.

Golden Lantern

1239 Royal St at Barracks ☎504/529-2860. Established neighborhood gay/drag bar, headquarters for the Southern Decadence Festival (see p.193), usually full with a crowd of devoted regulars. Open 24hr; happy hour daily 4–9pm, plus free food Friday 4–9pm.

▼ CAROUSEL BAR

French Quarter: Bourbon Street

Though you'd never guess it from the hype, there are two sides to world-renowned **Bourbon Street**. The tawdry, touristy, booze-swilled stretch spans the seven blocks from Canal to St Ann streets: a frat-pack cacophony of daiquiri stalls, novelty shops, and tired girlie bars offering "French style" entertainment. This self-contained enclave is best experienced after dark, when a couple – though by no means all – of its bars and clubs are worth a look, and the sheer mayhem takes on a bacchanalian life of its own. When the attraction of fighting your way through the crowds wanes, it's easy to dip out again into the quieter parallel streets to regain some sort of sanity. After St Ann, you come to a kind of crossroads beyond which Bourbon transforms into an appealing, predominantly gay, residential area, scattered with neighborhood bars, old-style corner stores, and local restaurants.

Hermann-Grima House

820 St Louis St at Bourbon. Mon–Fri tours every half-hour 10am–3.30pm. $6, $10 with the Gallier House (see p.81). Half a block above Bourbon Street, the 1832 Hermann-Grima House illustrates the lifestyle of two middle-class Creole families in antebellum New Orleans. Though in many ways a typically Federal mansion, the house's loggia and outside kitchen whisper of a lingering Creole sensibility. It was built for Samuel Hermann, a German-Jewish cotton and slave trader, who, following nationwide economic panic in 1837, was forced to sell it in 1844 to Judge Felix Grima. The Grimas lived here until the

▼ HERMANN-GRIMA HOUSE

The name Bourbon Street

Ironically, given its reputation, the street's name has nothing to do with booze. One of the first roads laid out by the city's planner Adrien de Pauger in 1721, Bourbon was named for the royal family of France, and only took on its current character during World War II, when a rash of strip clubs and bars opened to cater to soldiers passing through the port.

1920s, after which it became a women's hostel. Though tours skimp on contextual detail to dwell reverentially on replica antiques, they do at least give you time to wander around the rooms rather than trooping you past a succession of cordoned-off set pieces. Much of the furniture was made by prominent local craftsman Prudent Mallard; note especially the ornate bed with its characteristic egg motif, a visual pun on his surname. Creole cookery demonstrations are held in the kitchen every Thursday from October to May.

Bourbon-Orleans Hotel

The Bourbon-Orleans Hotel, on the corner of those two streets, stands on the site of the old Salle d'Orleans ballroom, which, in the antebellum era, was the grandest venue for the much-mythologized quadroon balls. Usually romanticized as glittering occasions where dashing white men had their hearts stolen by beautiful, dusky quadroon girls (one-quarter black, usually born to a white father and mulatto mother), the reality of the balls was less glamorous: put simply, these were dances where wealthy white planters and merchants were able to consort with poorer, mixed-race girls chaperoned by their mothers. Little would usually come of the encounters, but occasionally, under a formalized system

known as *plaçage*, a lucky few were set up in homes of their own, raising the children of their paramour, who would usually also be supporting a "respectable" white family.

The Historic Voodoo Museum

724 Dumaine St, between Bourbon and Royal. Daily 10am–dusk. $7.
A mesmerizing, if muffled, soundtrack of drumming and chanting introduces the intriguing little Historic Voodoo Museum. A ragbag collection of shrines, ceremonial objects, portraits, and *gris-gris* (spells or potions), the museum aims to debunk the myths that surround this often misunderstood spiritual practice – an intention undermined slightly by the spooky atmosphere, not to mention its resident Albino python, crumbling rat heads,

▼ VOODOO ON BOURBON STREET

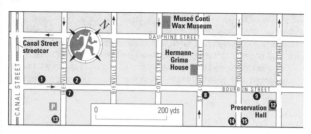

and desiccated bats. The gift shop sells *gris-gris* and voodoo dolls, and also offers readings and tours.

Lafitte's Blacksmith Shop

941 Bourbon St at St Philip. The alarmingly tumbledown Lafitte's Blacksmith Shop – now a great little bar – is one of the oldest buildings in the Quarter. Built around 1781, it's a typical early Creole cottage, with a steeply pitched roof (the dormers were a later addition); blotches of stucco on the walls have crumbled off to reveal its *briquette entre poteaux* construction (see p.194). According to legend, the shop was used as a cover for pirate brothers Jean and Pierre Lafitte, leaders of the "Baratarians," a thousand-strong band of smugglers who hid out in the Barataria swamps at the mouth of the Mississippi. Though the importation of slaves was outlawed in 1804, there was such a high demand for labor in the thriving colony that illegal slave smuggling was a lucrative racket, and it was in murky little cottages like these that plans were hatched and raids plotted.

Voodoo in New Orleans

Voodoo was brought to New Orleans by African slaves from the Caribbean, where tribal beliefs had been mixed with Catholicism, the official religion of the French colonies, to create a new cult based on spirit worship. French and, later, Spanish authorities tried to suppress the religion, but it continued to flourish among the city's black population, especially after 1809 when the ban was lifted on importation of slaves. Under American rule, the weekly slave gatherings at Congo Square (see p.113), which included ritual ceremonies, turned into a tourist attraction for whites, fueled by sensationalized reports of hypnotized white women dancing naked to the throbbing drum music.

New Orleans had many voodoo priestesses; the most famous was Marie Laveau, a hairdresser of African, white, and Native American blood, who was in high demand for her *gris-gris* – spells – which she prepared for wealthy Creoles and Americans, as well as Africans. Laveau died in 1881, after which another Marie, believed to be her daughter, continued to practice under her name. The legend of both Maries lives on, and their crumbling tombs are popular tourist attractions (see pp.115 & 116).

If you've got a serious interest in the religion, head for the voodoo museum or the Voodoo Spiritual Temple, 828 N Rampart St (☎504/522-9627), where the charismatic Priestess Miriam holds services, and offers tours and consultations.

Restaurants

Acme Oyster House

724 Iberville St at Bourbon
ⓣ504/522-5973. With its checked
tablecloths, neon signs, marble-
topped oyster bar, and fast,
smart-talking staff, this noisy
place has been *the* French
Quarter hangout for raw oysters
and ice-cold beer for nearly one
hundred years. A dozen briny
bivalves on the half-shell costs
just $6.99, or you can get them
fried for around $13. In season,
don't miss the fresh, buttery
mudbugs, boiled in a delicious,
pepper-hot stock. Or try the
gut-busting medley of gumbo,
jambalaya, and red beans and
rice with sausage – not the
finest in the city, but at a mere
$8.99 the price can't be beat.

Bistro at Maison de Ville

727 Toulouse St at Bourbon
ⓣ504/528-9206, ⓦwww
.maisondeville.com. Creole cuisine
and brasserie standards served
in a romantic little restaurant
linked to the historic hotel
(see p.178). It feels like an
old French bistro with its red
leather banquettes, bevelled glass
mirrors, and wooden floors, and
the seasonal menu concentrates
on the classics – sweetbreads,
rack of lamb, *moules-frîtes*, pan-
seared scallops, crème brûlée,
and so on. Prix-fixe options
include a three-course linch

for $20. Superb wine list.
Reservations advised.

Clover Grill

900 Bourbon St at Dumaine
ⓣ504/598-1010. Daily 24hr. Camp
all-night diner – "We love to fry
and it shows" – with counter
seating and a few booths, usually
crowded with a gay Bourbon
Street clientele filling up on
fries, burgers, omelettes, and
shakes. It's always lively and can
get rowdy: come for a post-
bar-crawl breakfast of waffles,
pancakes, or Froot Loops, then
sit back and enjoy the scene.
Great jukebox, too.

▼ CORNER LAUNDROMAT

▲ FELIX'S

Felix's Oyster House

739 Iberville St at Bourbon ☎504/522-4440. Just across the road from *Acme*, but less crowded, *Felix's* offers raw oysters on the half-shell just as fresh as its rival's and slightly cheaper, plus a broader range of tasty seafood dishes (oysters Rockefeller, oysters Bienville, seafood gumbo, oyster stew, and the like) in sedate – some might say subdued – surroundings.

Galatoire's

209 Bourbon St at Iberville ☎504/525-2021. Closed Mon. Tennessee Williams' favorite restaurant, this grand Creole establishment, with its dark wood, black-and-white tiled floor, ceiling fans, and old mirrors, is quintessentially New Orleans – elegant, relaxed, and not at all stuffy. It's best at lunchtime, on Friday or Sunday especially, when locals spend long, convivial hours gorging on turtle soup, oysters Rockefeller, shrimp *rémoulade*, and filet mignon. Finish with a fragrant café brulot, prepared tableside. Reservations are taken only for the less atmospheric, upstairs room, so arrive early

and be prepared to wait. Jackets required after 5pm and all day Sunday.

Redfish Grill

115 Bourbon St at Iberville ☎504/598-1200. Casual, Ralph Brennan-owned fish restaurant. The brash ragwashed walls and metallic palm trees are a bit offputting, but the good-value food isn't bad at all; at just $11 the Bourbon Street Sampler – coconut shrimp, barbecue oysters, alligator sausage, and crabcakes – is ample for two. At dinner they offer six different fresh grilled fish, served in a variety of ways including crusted with pecans, andouille, or sweet potato. The desserts are fabulous.

Bars

Café Lafitte in Exile and Balcony Bar

901 Bourbon St at Dumaine ☎504/522-8397, ⓦwww.lafittes.com. In continuous operation since the 1950s, this rambunctious, welcoming gay men's bar is a much-loved favorite, with a

▼ CAFÉ LAFITTE IN EXILE

▲ LAFITTE'S BLACKSMITH SHOP

balcony that becomes party central during Mardi Gras. Open 24hr; various promotions and happy hours, with karaoke on Wed.

The Dungeon

738 Toulouse St at Bourbon

☎504/523-5530. Hidden away down a spooky side-alley, this Stygian hideout is a maze of nooks and crannies lit only by the dimmest red lightbulbs: skulls, cages, and cobwebs abound. With a dancefloor and three bars, it features good specials and occasional Goth and fetish nights. Open Tues–Sun from midnight; $3 cover on weekends.

Lafitte's Blacksmith Shop

941 Bourbon St at St Philip St

☎504/523-0066. Dim, ancient bar frequented by artists, writers (how they see by the candlelight remains a mystery), and lots of stray tourists. One of the oldest buildings in the Quarter, bought by notorious pirate Jean Lafitte in 1809, it's a tumbledown shack with beamed ceilings and a blackened brick fireplace (where Lafitte's treasure is said to be stashed). At night, a gloriously cheesy piano player pounds out cocktail-lounge standards to a gaggle of drunken reprobates – there's a patio for those who want a quieter time.

Pat O'Brien's

718 St Peter St at Bourbon

☎504/525-4823. Opened during Prohibition (but in this location since 1942), this is probably the most famous bar in New Orleans and, for many, an obligatory stop on the Bourbon Street circuit. It's a vast, noisy complex, spilling over with drunken tourists, most of whom are guzzling the requisite Hurricane cocktail, served in 29oz hurricane-lamp glasses. There's a huge patio, complete with kitsch multicolored water-and-flame fountains, and a raucous "dueling" piano bar – surprisingly, the small side-room attracts a friendly local crowd on Sunday afternoons.

▲ PRESERVATION HALL

Live music and clubs

735

735 Bourbon St at St Ann ☎504/581-6740, ☞www.club735.com. They say "You'll forget it's Bourbon Street" in this edgy enclave where the pierced and fancy-dress set dance to alternative, electro, retro, trance, and house. Plus cult movies, themed nights, and regular drinks specials. Cover varies.

Bourbon Pub/ Parade

801 Bourbon St at St Ann ☎504/529-2107, ☞www.bourbonpub .com. Noisy, sweaty video-bar and club at the heart of the Quarter's gay scene. The *Bourbon Happy Hour* is hugely popular, while *Parade*, upstairs, offers frequent foam parties (where "dirty boys get clean and clean boys get dirty"), drag nights, and talent contests. Cover varies.

Chris Owens

500 Bourbon St at St Louis ☎504/523-6400, ☞www.chrisowensclub.com. Chris Owens' one-woman variety show brings you Bourbon Street bawdiness at its old-fashioned best. Glitzy, spangly, and unashamedly camp, Chris has been a fixture here since 1967, high-kicking and grinding her way through Latin, Las Vegas, and pop standards, and shows no sign of stopping.

▼ MIXOLOGY, BOURBON STREET-STYLE

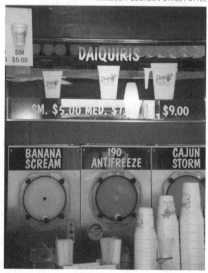

Shows 8.30pm and 10pm, with a Latin disco afterwards.

Oz

800 Bourbon St at St Ann ☎504/593-9491, ⑩www.oznewmorleans.com.
High-tech gay disco with a wild balcony. It's opposite the *Bourbon Pub* and similarly lively, with drag nights, talent shows, fabulous go-go boys, bingo, and game shows. Cover varies.

Preservation Hall

726 St Peter St at Bourbon ☎504/522-2841, ⑩www.preservationhall.com.
Long lauded as the best place in New Orleans to hear traditional jazz, this unbelievably shabby room has no bar, air-conditioning, or toilets, and just a handful of hard benches for seating. Though the building is as old as it looks, the *Hall* itself opened in the 1960s, and has changed little since. The dereliction is a bit hokey perhaps, but the music, played by old pros, is outstanding. It's always bursting at the seams with tourists, and lines form well before doors open; sets, each about 45min with 15min gaps, run 8.30–11.45pm. The $5 cover allows you to stay as long as you like, and people move out steadily, so you're bound to get a seat in the end.

French Quarter: Above Bourbon Street

Above Bourbon Street, the French Quarter becomes markedly more peaceful and residential, tourists outnumbered by locals dog-walking, jogging, picking up provisions in corner groceries, or chatting on stoops. These quiet streets are fringed by some of the Quarter's finest vernacular architecture: narrow shotguns and Creole cottages, the hues of hand-tinted antique photos, standing flush with the sidewalk. Small courtyards are tended lovingly, with myrtle and magnolia blossoms tangling over cast-iron fences and fountains tinkling at the heart of hidden patios. There are a number of popular gay bars, upscale restaurants, and bookstores above Bourbon, but, as you head toward Tremé (see p.113), these streets can be eerily isolated after dark; if you feel at all nervous, restrict your explorations to the daytime.

Musée Conti Wax Museum

917 Conti St at Dauphine. Mon–Sat 10am–5.30pm, Sun noon–5pm. $6.75. This delightfully old-fashioned museum tells the story of New Orleans through a series of lurid tableaux, augmented by sound recordings (check out those great French accents), that include the Battle of New Orleans, Napoleon pontificating in his bathtub, a slave auction, wild-eyed voodoo dancers, and a hard-faced, whip-wielding Madame LaLaurie (see p.81). The grand finale comes, apropos of nothing, in the

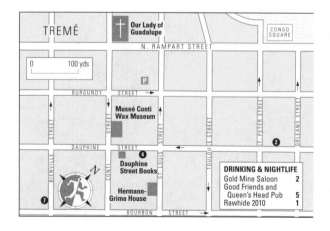

DRINKING & NIGHTLIFE
Gold Mine Saloon   2
Good Friends and
   Queen's Head Pub   5
Rawhide 2010   1

▲ MADAME LALAURIE AT THE WAX MUSEUM

Haunted Dungeon, where encounters with sundry ghouls are backed by recorded shrieking and wailing.

Shops

Dauphine Street Books

410 Dauphine St at Conti ℡504/529-2333. Closed Tues and Wed. A gem of a store, with piles of used and new books, especially strong on local fiction, history, photography, and Latin American translations.

Kaboom Books

915 Barracks St at Dauphine ℡504/529-5780. Kaboom's floor plan helps you negotiate the narrow aisles, which are stuffed full of used volumes including fiction (lots of crime), drama, travel, film, biographies, and photography. It's strong on history, especially of the South, and has a good African-American section.

Restaurants

Bayona

430 Dauphine St at Conti ℡504/525-4455. Closed for lunch Sat, closed Sun. Splendid, romantic, and relaxed restaurant in a seventeenth-century Creole cottage with a lovely courtyard. Local celebrity chef Susan Spicer creates creative, unfussy "Global Cuisine," using organic ingredients and giving local

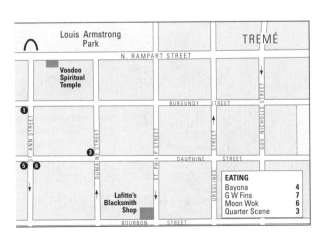

EATING
Bayona	4
G W Fins	7
Moon Wok	6
Quarter Scene	3

▲ BAYONA

G W Fins

808 Bienville at Bourbon
℡504/581-3467, ⓦwww
.gwfins.com. Dinner only.
Fish lovers with cash
to spend will adore this
sophisticated restaurant,
which flies in daily its
fresh seafood from around
the world. The changing
menu is superb – try the
mouthwatering lobster
dumplings, horseradish-
crusted drum with truffle
sauce, or smoked sizzling
oysters – the service classy,
and you can get more
than 70 wines by the glass. That
said, if you've got just a night or
two in New Orleans you may
prefer a more local experience
– GW Fins, as fine as it is, could
be in any big city in the USA.

Moon Wok

800 Dauphine St at St Ann ℡504/523-
6910. Closed Wed. Inexpensive
Chinese food – unusual in
the Quarter – dished up in
modest, Deco-ish surroundings.
At lunch, it's busy with frugal
locals and a few stray tourists,

dishes an Asian, Southwestern,
or European twist – grilled
shrimp with black-bean
cake and cilantro sauce, say.
The simple garlic soup and
sweetbreads are outstanding,
and the 250-plus wine list is
excellent. Make sure to go for
lunch, when you can get three
courses for less than $25, or a
dazzling grilled cashew butter,
duck, and pepper jelly sandwich
with crisp apple slaw for a
staggeringly low $9.

▼ SHOTGUN HOUSE

▲ KNOCK, KNOCK. SHOES THERE?

while evening diners are usually young and hip, filling up before a big night out. The long menu includes all the Asian–American standards as well as more unusual choices like crawfish in black bean sauce. Lunch combos (11am–3pm) are good value at $6.95 (rising to $8.95 after 3pm). BYOB.

Quarter Scene

900 Dumaine St at Dauphine ☎504/522-7533. During the day this casual, gay-owned restaurant lures you in with its plants and statuary, mismatched tables, and splashy paintings lining the red-brick walls. It's best for breakfast and brunch, with lots of eggs Benedict, fruit, and pancake combinations; at night, flickering in the candlelight, it becomes sweetly romantic. The dinner menu, however, isn't terribly exciting, based on Creole standards, though specials do venture into Asian and Caribbean territory. BYOB.

Bars

Good Friends and Queen's Head Pub

740 Dauphine St at St Ann ☎504/566-7191, ⊛www.goodfriendsbar.com.

This good-natured gay bar has a cozy, neighborhood feel, with a working fireplace and pool tables. The mock-English ambience at the *Queen's Head*, upstairs, extends to the much-used dartboard and a popular piano singalong on Sunday afternoon (4–8pm). Regular drinks specials and party events.

Rawhide 2010

740 Burgundy St at St Ann ☎504/525-8106, ⊛www.rawhide2010.com. The Quarter's only leather and denim bar, *Rawhide 2010* keeps going around the clock. During Mardi Gras, there are lots of special events and promotions, including beer specials for tattooed customers, and a daily happy hour 4–9pm.

Clubs

Gold Mine Saloon

705 Dauphine St at Orleans ☎504/586-0745. This unpretentious local bar, with its pool tables and foosball, transforms into a heaving mixed dance club at night, with disco, techno, and old school house. Poetry nights, on Thursday, pull an avant-garde crowd. Cover varies.

The Mississippi River

A resonant, romantic, and extraordinary physical presence, **the Mississippi River** is New Orleans' lifeblood and its raison d'être. About half a mile wide, it writhes through the city like an out-of-control snake, swelling against the man-made levees as it courses toward the Gulf of Mexico. By the early nineteenth century, New Orleans became a major meeting point for riverboats, ocean-going ships, and foreign vessels. Joining them were bands of pirates and, by the 1840s, hundreds of steamboats. With their puffing chimneys, fancy galleries, and enormous paddlewheels, these "floating palaces" poured even more goods, travelers, and card-sharks into the city. More recently, a couple of downtown parks, plazas, and riverside walks, accessible from the French Quarter and the CBD, have focused attention back onto the waterfront, capitalizing on its magnetic appeal.

Washington Artillery Park and the Moonwalk

Directly across Decatur from Jackson Square, Washington Artillery Park is a rather grand name for a small, elevated strip of concrete, reached by steps, that gives superb photo opportunities of the square and St Louis Cathedral, and, in the other direction, of the Mississippi.

Descend the steps on the river side, walk through the break in the concrete flood walls, over the riverfront streetcar tracks, and up another flight of steps, and you'll find the Moonwalk, a riverfront promenade named for "Moon" Landrieu, mayor from 1970 to 1978. It's a great spot, especially at sunset, when its iron benches fill with tourists gazing at the panorama upriver to the Mississippi River Bridge and, downriver, to the wharves that begin at Governor Nicholls Street. Gulls dip and dive in front of you, in the vain hope of plucking catfish out of the whirling eddies, while ships battle against the savage current at Algiers Point, the sharpest bend in the entire river. Safe enough during the day, the Moonwalk is best avoided late at night.

Woldenberg Park

Long, thin Woldenberg Park curves upriver from the end of Toulouse Street to the Aquarium of the Americas. It's a good place to sprawl on the grass with a picnic, watching the tugs and towboats, barges and naval tankers on the Mississippi, and the constant stream of tourists between the aquarium and the French Quarter.

Aquarium of the Americas

Sun–Thurs 9.30am–6pm, Fri & Sat 9.30am–7pm; $15, children $8; IMAX $8/$5; aquarium and IMAX $19/$12; aquarium and Audubon Zoo (see p.145) $20/$11; aquarium, zoo, and cruise $34/$16.50; aquarium, IMAX, and

River tours

Apart from the sheer delight of churning along one of the world's greatest rivers on a big old sternwheeler, a short cruise on the Mississippi offers a fascinating glimpse into the workings of the nation's most important waterway. Some take you as far as Chalmette, riverfront site of the 1815 Battle of New Orleans.

If you're after a cruise plain and simple, the three-deck *Natchez* sternwheeler steamboat – heralded by its hauntingly off-key calliope tunes, which float through the French Quarter about thirty minutes before the boat sets off – is by far the best choice. It leaves twice a day from the Toulouse Street wharf behind Jackson Brewery and heads seven or so miles downriver, turning back near the Chalmette Battlefield. You can sit on deck or lunch inside on fried chicken and red beans, with live Dixieland jazz accompaniment (daily 11.30am & 2.30pm; 2hr; $18.50, $25.50 with lunch; dinner jazz cruise 6pm, departs 7pm; 2hr; $51 with food, $30 without; kids half-price in all cases; ☏504/586-8777).

Though less atmospheric, the *John James Audubon* riverboat is a great option if you want to combine a cruise with a trip to the aquarium (see p.98), or Audubon Zoo (p.145), or both. Cruises leave daily from the aquarium at 10am, noon, 2pm, and 4pm, and from the zoo an hour later ($17 round-trip; $25.75 with aquarium, $22.25 with zoo, $34 with both; $40.50 with both plus IMAX; children half-price; ☏504/586-8777).

To see Chalmette, take the *Creole Queen* paddlewheeler (10.30am & 2pm; 2hr 30min; $19, $11 children; $26/$17 with lunch; ☏504/524-0814). It leaves from the Plaza d'España. Tickets for all cruises are sold at riverside booths behind Jackson Brewery and the aquarium.

PLACES The Mississippi River

zoo $27/$15; aquarium, IMAX, zoo, and cruise $40.50/$20.50. Entering New Orleans' superb aquarium, through a clear tunnel where tropical fish, flapping rays, and hawksbill turtles whirl above and around you, brings you into a vast place where different environments are recreated in lively detail. The steamy Amazonian rainforest demonstrates how monstrous fish, grown fat on the river's bounty, develop sensitive whiskers and an acute sense of hearing in order to make their way through the silty, muddy water. Rainbow macaws flap

▼ AQUARIUM OF THE AMERICAS

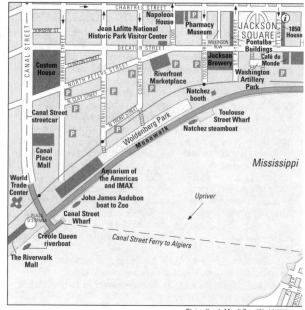

Blaine Kern's Mardi Gras World ▼

above you as you cross a tree-top pathway, while thumbnail-sized poisoned-dart frogs and bird-eating spiders lurk menacingly in glass enclosures. The Mississippi Delta, meanwhile, complete with its own mossy cypress trees, features one of New Orleans' white alligators (see p.145), ancient paddlefish, and the unnerving giant flathead catfish, who feed on geese, ducks, and even dogs.

Be sure to make time for the sharks, which range from weird-looking Australian wobbegongs to leathery nurse sharks – which you're encouraged to stroke – and the infinitesimal jellyfish that sparkle in the dark blue water like tiny Christmas-tree lights. And on no account miss the seahorse exhibit, where you'll find the leafy sea dragon, nonchalantly disguised as a tangle of foliage, and the strange weedy sea

dragon, hovering in the kelp like some arthritic Dr Seuss creature. The five-story IMAX theater shows the usual overblown epics of mountaineering, space exploration, and other derring-do.

Plaza d'España and the Riverwalk Mall

The sunken Plaza d'España sits nudged in between the river and New Orleans' woefully drab World Trade Center. A large, circular space tiled with Spanish coats of arms, it feels rather European with its piped Spanish music and huge fountain, and makes a nice place to hang out, especially in the cool of early evening.

From the plaza you can enter the half-mile-long Riverwalk Mall, which is usually scuttling with big-spending weekenders and conference delegates

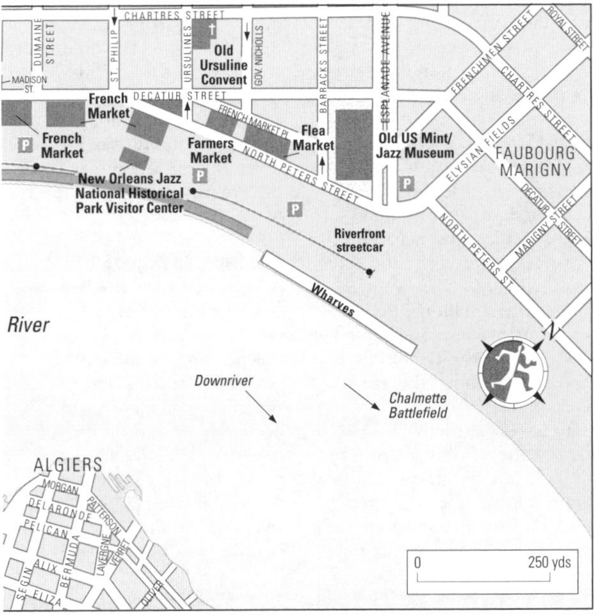

The map shows streets and landmarks including:

- CHARTRES STREET
- DUMAINE STREET
- ST PHILIP
- MADISON ST
- URSULINES
- GOV NICHOLLS
- DECATUR STREET
- BARRACKS STREET
- ESPLANADE AVENUE
- FRENCHMEN STREET
- CHARTRES STREET
- ROYAL STREET
- 1 Old Ursuline Convent
- French Market
- FRENCH MARKET
- Farmers Market
- NORTH PETERS STREET
- Flea Market
- Old US Mint/ Jazz Museum
- ELYSIAN FIELDS
- DECATUR ST
- FAUBOURG MARIGNY
- French Market
- New Orleans Jazz National Historical Park Visitor Center
- Riverfront streetcar
- NORTH PETERS ST
- MARIGNY STREET
- Wharves
- River
- Downriver
- Chalmette Battlefield
- ALGIERS
- MORGAN
- DELARONDE
- PELICAN
- PATTERSON
- LAVERGNE
- OLIVIER
- ALIX
- BERMUDA
- SEGUIN
- ELIZA
- N
- 0   250 yds

scooping up suitcase-fulls of souvenirs as they rush between the convention center and the French Quarter. Even if you're not shopping, it's worth strolling along the mall's outdoor promenade, which is raised above river-level and dotted with illuminating historical plaques.

Chalmette Battlefield

Daily 9am–5pm. Free. About six miles downriver from the city, off Hwy-46, the Chalmette Battlefield National Historical Park was the site of the Battle of New Orleans, the final skirmish of the War of 1812. In 1814, having captured Washington, DC, the British turned their sights to the Gulf. On December 23, British General Edward Pakenham and his nine thousand Redcoats arrived five miles downriver of the city, to be met by Andrew Jackson's

▼ PLAZA D'ESPAÑA

five-thousand-strong volunteer force of Creoles, Anglo-American adventurers, free men of color, Baratarian pirates, and Native Americans. On January 8, 1815, after a battle lasting minutes, Jackson's men routed their opponents. The death toll came to seven hundred Redcoats, and just a dozen or so Americans. Ironically, the battle, from which Jackson went on to become a national hero, was unnecessary: news soon reached the city that the Treaty of Ghent had already ended the war in December 1814.

Today the battle is commemorated by a 110-foot obelisk and an interpretive exhibit in the visitor center. Park rangers give short talks for visitors who have arrived on the *Creole Queen* river cruises (see p.99); if you've come under your own steam you'll have more time to wander freely around the site (a loop of a mile and a half) and to watch the thirty-minute video that details the events leading up to the War of 1812.

The ferry to Algiers

A ferry ride from the bottom of Canal Street brings you within five minutes or so – depending on the current – to the west bank and the old shipbuilding community of Algiers. Seen from the lofty heights of the *360°* bar (see p.104), the ferry looks tiny, swirling alarmingly with the river's flow – the Mississippi is at its deepest (nearly 200ft) here,

The Big Muddy

North America's principal waterway, the Mississippi – the name comes from the Algonquin words for "big" and "river" – is the third longest river in the world after the Nile and the Amazon. Starting as a 12ft deep and 18ft wide stream just ninety miles south of the Canadian border in Minnesota, it twists its way 2348 miles to the mouth at the Gulf of Mexico, 217 river miles (65 miles as the crow flies) from New Orleans. On its way it takes in more than one hundred tributaries and drains 41 percent of continental America, an area of more than a million square miles.

The Big Muddy – so nicknamed because it carries 2lb of dirt for every 1000lb of water – is one of the busiest commercial rivers in the world and one of the least conventional. Instead of widening toward its mouth, like most rivers, the Mississippi grows narrower and deeper. The Mississippi is also, in the words of Mark Twain, who spent four years as a riverboat pilot, "the crookedest river in the world." As it weaves and curls its way extravagantly along its channel, it continually cuts through narrow necks of land to shape and reshape oxbow lakes, meander scars, cut-offs, and marshy backwaters. Some engineers predict that eventually the river will desert its present channel altogether and find a shorter route to the sea, bypassing New Orleans entirely.

The Mississippi's propensity to flood is a particularly serious threat to low-lying New Orleans, which at its highest point reaches just 15ft above sea level. Since disastrous flooding in the 1920s wiped out entire communities throughout the Mississippi Valley, the federal government has been responsible for a wide range of protective measures all along the river. In New Orleans, the levee is backed by a series of flood walls. Recently these have been rendered less necessary with the building of the Spillway, which, when the river reaches dangerous levels, automatically drains into Lake Pontchartrain – to the dismay of conservationists, who claim that it pours polluted water into the lake.

▲ RIVER TOURS

and the current fierce, churning furiously around the extreme bend in the river. Even if you don't disembark, the views of both banks – especially at sunset – and the chance to see the river traffic up close make it well worth a ride in itself. Ferries leave every 30min: from Canal Street between 6am and midnight, and from Algiers between 5.45am and 11.45pm. Pedestrians ride free; it's $1 each way for bikes and cars.

Algiers

Settled a couple of years after New Orleans was established on the east bank, Algiers was entirely separate from the early city. The origins of its name are obscure, though, as a major eighteenth-century disembarkation point for the slave boats, it may have been named for the African slave port. In 1819, the first shipyard opened on the point, and settlement increased; the coming of the railways and the development of the shipbuilding industry during the Civil War led to further growth, and in 1870 the city was incorporated into New Orleans.

Just as across the river, Algiers' saloons spawned some of the city's earliest jazz music, often created by freed slaves who had played in brass bands on the local plantations. Algiers fell into decline after the 1920s, and was touched little by the oil boom and subsequent modernizations inflicted on the east bank.

The main attraction here is the Mardi Gras museum; before catching the ferry back, take time to climb up onto the levee, from where the downtown skyline is at its most photogenic.

Blaine Kern's Mardi Gras World

233 Newton St at Brooklyn. Daily 9.30am–4.30pm, closed the two weeks before Mardi Gras. $13.50. The free bus waiting at the Algiers ferry terminal will whisk you off to the cavernous "dens" of Blaine Kern's Mardi Gras World, a working facility where you can see artists preparing, constructing, and painting the overblown papier-mâché floats used in the carnival parades. Kern's team makes floats for around forty or so of the krewes, including super krewe Bacchus, whose enormous King Kong family, Bacchawhoppa whale and Bacchagator – a white alligator, like those in the city's zoo and aquarium – hibernate here for most of the year. It's a surreal experience

▲ MARDI GRAS MARILYN

wandering these paint-splattered warehouses, past piles of dusty, grimacing has-beens from parades gone by – limbless cartoon characters lolling over caved-in crawfish, superstars snuggling with presidents. In keeping with the carnival spirit, there are plenty of opportunities to dress up, fool about, and take photos – you're encouraged to try on Marilyn Monroe and George Bush papier-mâché heads, velvet cloaks, and towering plumed headdresses

– and, at the start of the tour, each visitor gets free coffee and a slice of carnival King cake. For more on Mardi Gras, see p.162.

Shops

The Riverwalk Mall

1 Poydras St, on the Mississippi
☏504/522-1555. Bustling, touristy mall running along the river from Julia Street to the Plaza d'España. Its three stories house 150 shops, including, among the souvenir stores and Mardi Gras emporia, chains such as Banana Republic, Gap, Abercrombie and Fitch, and Footlocker. There's also a food court dominated by local favorites (seafood, fried chicken, po-boys) and including a *Café du Monde* (see p.58).

Bars

360º

World Trade Center, Canal Street at the River. There's something disarming about entering the marble, flag-lined lobby of New Orleans' WTC and ascending

▼ ENJOYING THE VIEW AT 360º

in the elevator past office complexes to this revolving bar on the 33rd floor. With its fancy cocktails, leopard-skin prints, and plush chaise longues, *360°* tries hard; the effect tends more toward the kitsch than the hip however, and it always seems slightly gone to seed, especially during the day – which is, of course, part of its charm. That, and the unbeatable views. Along with miles and miles of the broad river, including the startling bend around Algiers, one ninety-minute revolution spans the tiny congested grid of the Quarter, the roofs of the CBD towers, and the poker-straight channel of Canal Street. At night, when you'll need to dress up, the bar turns into a dance club, crammed with groups of single thirtysomethings.

Faubourg Marigny and Bywater

Crossing Esplanade from the French Quarter brings you to **Faubourg Marigny**, a happening, low-rent area of Creole cottages and shotguns populated by artists, musicians, and sundry bohemians. The Faubourg is named for the Creole Bernard de Marigny, a millionaire roué and gambler who, in 1808 and in drastic debt, divided his vast plantation into lots and sold them off. Today it's a hugely popular place to hang out at night, and the area's hipster credentials are slowly being passed on to its neighbor, residential **Bywater**, another up-and-coming artists' district which offers some great restaurants and bars. Though the Faubourg is gentrifying, it's best not to wander too far beyond the blocks around Decatur and Frenchmen, the district's main drag and nightlife strip, especially after dark. And to get to Bywater, always cab it.

Esplanade Avenue

The downriver boundary of the French Quarter, Esplanade Avenue is a ravishing, if somewhat down-at-heel boulevard, lined with huge, twisted live oaks and decaying Italianate mansions once populated by the city's free women of color and their French-speaking families. At the end of the nineteenth century, this was the grandest residential street in the declining Creole city; these days its faded glamour is part of its charm.

▼ ESPLANADE AVENUE

▲ FAUBOURG MARIGNY ART & BOOKS

Z'otz

2003 Royal St at Touro
℡504/943-9689. Daily 24hr. With its ripped velvet sofas, tatty decapitated dolls, ancient candlesticks, and goldfish swimming freely in the bath, this friendly, decrepit little place pulls an arty, pierced, Faubourg crowd, who hang out for hours chatting, playing Scrabble, and checking email. Along with breakfast and snacks, you can get good coffee, a dizzying array of herbal teas, and hookahs in a variety of flavors.

Shops

Faubourg Marigny Art & Books

600 Frenchmen St at Chartres
℡504/947-3700. The city's oldest gay and lesbian bookstore, selling novels, art books, travel guides, regional titles, postcards, and calendars. They host occasional readings and live music events.

Cafés

Café Rose Nicaud

628 Frenchmen St at Chartres
℡504/949-3300. This comfortable, spacious neighborhood coffee bar, decorated in warm reds and ochres, is popular with local intellectuals and musicians, who linger for ages over cappuccinos, herbal teas, and sandwiches, reading, writing, and talking, either at the marble-topped tables or in the capacious leather armchairs. They also serve light lunches, with salads and paninis.

Restaurants

Adolfo's

611 Frenchmen St at Chartres
℡504/948-3800. Dinner only, closed Sun. Gutsy Italian-Creole food in a cozy room tucked above the *Apple Barrel* bar. Decorated with Christmas-tree lights, candles, and splashy art on the wood-paneled walls, it's the perfect setting for enjoying robust pasta and seafood. Non-pasta meals start with a tasty spaghetti appetizer; to follow, choose from entrées such as pansautéed softshell crab stuffed with shrimp, or redfish with crawfish étouffé. Pasta dishes include cannelloni stuffed with crabmeat, sweetcorn, and ricotta.

Elizabeth's

601 Gallier St at Chartres, Bywater
℡504/944-9272. Tues–Sat; breakfast & lunch only. Even *Elizabeth's* logo, a cheery pig, can't prepare you for the size of the portions at this fabulous diner. Pulling in a loyal crowd of local artists and blue-collar workers with its

tasty food and low prices, for visitors it's a perfect place to take a break from the Quarter. Breakfast (till 10.30am) will set you up for the day; try a po-boy overstuffed with scrambled egg, sausage, and cheese. They do po-boys for lunch (from 10.30am), too, as well as unbelievably good specials ($6.50 or so) such as crawfish cheesecake or boudin-stuffed chicken breast with greens and rice. No credit cards, and no cell phones.

Feelings Café

2600 Chartres St at Franklin
☎504/945-2222, ®www.feelingscafe
.com. Mon–Thurs, Sat dinner only.
Lovely, romantic restaurant in a complex of restored plantation buildings with a shady brick courtyard. Both the old-world New Orleans/Caribbean ambience and the classic French Creole food – lots of shrimp, seafood, steak, and duck – are delicious. Prices aren't low – a meal of softshell crab with avocado butter followed by Gulf fish with Dijon mustard and shrimp will set you back about $30 before tax and gratuity.

Marisol

437 Esplanade Ave at Frenchmen
☎504/943-1912, ®www
.marisolrestaurant.com. Closed Mon
& Tues. The long menu changes daily at this elegant French-American bistro, but typical choices include Hudson Valley foie gras served simply with

▼ MARISOL

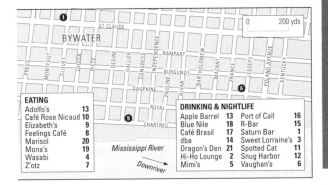

cracked black pepper and sea salt; potato-crusted Atlantic skate with squid ink *spaetzle*; and grilled pork Porterhouse with rock shrimp-manchego cheese stuffing. It's all delicious, if pricey; if you're on a budget, feast on tasty tapas (Wed–Fri 5–7pm) in the pretty courtyard for around $4 a go. The website also offers frequent money-off deals.

Mona's

504 Frenchmen St at Decatur ☎504/949-4115. Popular, airy, no-frills restaurant attached to a Middle Eastern grocery. The food – kebabs, flatbread pizzas, beef kibby, split red lentil soup – is wonderfully fresh and zingy, with lots of non-meat choices. At $7.95 the delicious vegetable platter, with hummus, babaganoush, tabbouleh, and falafel, is a steal, but you can't go wrong whatever you choose.

Wasabi

900 Frenchmen St at Burgundy ☎504/943-9433. Closed lunch Sat & Sun. No-fuss, laid-back neighborhood favorite, serving reliable sushi dinners from $15 ($9 at lunchtime). *À la carte* choices include tasty curried mussels, gyoza noodle soup, and a good selection of sushi rolls.

Bars

Apple Barrel

609 Frenchmen St at Chartres ☎504/949-9399. Tiny place beneath *Adolfo's* restaurant. Its cozy, pub-like atmosphere (there's even a darts board, though the darts went astray years ago) is a little incongruous on this supercool stretch, but it holds its own with a core group of laid-back regulars and drop-ins from the Frenchmen Street bar-hop circuit. Occasional live music.

dba

618 Frenchmen St at Chartres ☎504/942-3731. This slick bar sashayed into town in 2000 flashing its big-city credentials (the original *dba* opened in New York) and a choice of bottled beers that leaves most local bars reeling. It's not very New Orleans, but the drinks are good, if pricey, with more than twenty draught premium beers on tap, classy cocktails, and a range of spirits. Live music nightly.

Mimi's

2601 Royal St at Franklin ☎504/942-0690. Its location beyond the Frenchmen strip means that *Mimi's* stays pretty local, with a lively, cool crowd of creative types from Bywater. There's a good late-night tapas bar upstairs with wines from Spain, Portugal, and Latin America, and they host regular tango dances (with free lessons).

Port of Call

838 Esplanade Ave at Dauphine ☎504/523-0120. Known hereabouts for its fantastically juicy fresh burgers, *Port of Call* is an unpretentious drinking hole haunted by a noisy mix of Quarterites, Faubourg denizens, and in-the-know tourists, who put the world to rights around the large wooden bar or at small tables. A scattering of grubby nautical accoutrements is the only concession to style – this place is the archetype of a guileless, classic American bar. Don't miss the eclectic jukebox.

R-Bar

1431 Royal St at Kerlerec ☎504/948-7499. The quirky decor at this attitude-free bar – Buddhist prayer flags, peeling bordello mirrors on the red walls, 1970s armchairs, and the like – gives *R-Bar* an edge, making it popular with a convivial twentysomething set that

▼ R-BAR

includes visitors staying at the guesthouse upstairs. The pool table is played by some of the coolest sharks in town.

Saturn Bar

3067 St Claude Ave at Clouet, Bywater ☎504/949-7532. An extraordinary, junk-filled neighborhood dive that has to be seen to be believed. Its decrepitude gives it a funky New Orleans cachet, with easy-going regulars – artists, intellectuals, and off-duty service-industry workers – joined by wandering cats, dogs, and all manner of lost souls. The jukebox is great, too. Closes midnight.

Live music and clubs

Blue Nile

532 Frenchmen St at Decatur ☎504/948-2583, ⊛www.bluenilemusic.com. This battered old bar/music venue has seen a few name changes over the years – but, with its dark corners, hippyish starlit ceiling, and large dancefloor, it remains a likable stalwart on the Frenchmen strip. Nightly Latin, jazz, brass, funk, reggae, and tango. Free, or low cover.

Café Brasil

2100 Chartres St at Frenchmen ☎504/949-0851. Minimalist club at the center of the Faubourg scene. It's known for its eclectic world music (Latin, jazz, klezmer, reggae) and poetry readings, and there's a small adjoining bar lined with funky artworks. The huge windows make it feel very open, and the young, mixed, gorgeous crowd tends to spill onto Frenchmen Street, creating a lively block party. Cover varies.

Dragon's Den

435 Esplanade Ave at Frenchmen ☎504/949-1750. Tucked above a pretty, but mediocre, Thai restaurant in a crumbling townhouse, this opium-den-style bar/club is a favorite of local bright young things. While there is some seating on the perilously decrepit balcony, most people loll on the velvet floor cushions, crowd the low tables, or dance like demons next to the tiny stage. Music is a mixed bag of acoustic, avant-garde, and brass bands. Cover varies.

Hi-Ho Lounge

2239 St Claude at Elysian Fields ☎504/947-9344, ⊛www.hiholounge .com. Painfully hip club on the fringes of Tremé and the back end of the Faubourg, attracting in-the-know groovers for everything from blues, jazz, and alternative rock to drum'n'bass and house DJ nights.

Snug Harbor

626 Frenchmen St at Royal ☎504/949 -0696, ⊛www.snugjazz.com. Daily 5pm–2am. Sophisticated, prestigious jazz club in a small, two-story space packed tight with tables and chairs. Regulars include Astral Project, who play cool modern jazz, drum maestro Johnny Vidacovich, Charmaine Neville, and pianist Ellis Marsalis. The kitchen, serving Creole standards, closes at 11pm (midnight Fri & Sat), but the bar, from where you can hear the gigs – and watch them, on the tiny closed-circuit TV– stays open late. Shows 9pm and 11pm; cover $8–25.

Spotted Cat

623 Frenchmen St at Royal ☎504/943-3887. With a nightly menu of roots music, this cozy little bar has become the place to see the

▲ COREY HENRY AT BLUE NILE

New Orleans Jazz Vipers, whose high-octane percussionless twist on jubilant trad jazz is impossible not to dance to. No cover.

Sweet Lorraine's

1931 St Claude Ave at Touro ☎504/945-9654, ⊛www.sweetlorrainesjazzclub .com. This classy venue has established itself as a top spot for contemporary jazz. The room is small, but musicians love to play here, certain of an enthusiastic response. Plus black poetry nights, comedy, and jam sessions. Cover varies.

Vaughan's

4229 Dauphine St at Lesseps, Bywater ☎504/947-5562. Neighborhood bar that fills to bursting on Thursday, when the hugely popular local trumpeter Kermit Ruffins plays jubilant jazz trumpet with his Barbecue Swingers band. It's all very convivial, with the band crammed against the hard-dancing audience – a mixed bunch of high-spirited college students, the players' friends and family, and other musicians; between sets, help yourself to all-you-can-eat beans and rice from a massive pot. Cover $10 (Thurs only).

Rampart Street and Tremé

Just footsteps from the French Quarter, the residential neighborhood of Tremé – bounded by Canal, Rampart, Broad, and St Bernard streets – is the oldest African-American community in the United States. Many of New Orleans' most enduring cultural and artistic forms, among them jazz music – born from the Sunday slave gatherings in Congo Square and developed in the "sporting houses" of Storyville, the area's long-defunct red-light district – jazz funerals, and Second Line parades, were born here at the end of the nineteenth century, and the strong street culture remains as vibrant as ever. After the 1960s, when financial decline, drug problems and violent crime blighted the area, Tremé became a no-go enclave for visitors, and though the district has started to shed its dismal image, there's still some way to go before it feels entirely safe. Keep your wits about you, take a cab if you are in any doubt, and always take a cab at night.

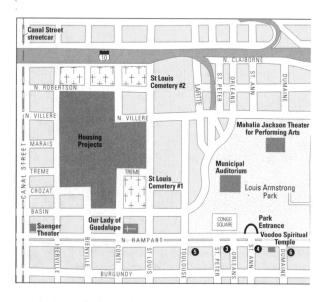

Rampart Street

For decades, North Rampart Street, the broad, run-down commercial strip that separates Tremé from the French Quarter, was depicted – by locals and guidebooks alike – as a barrier not to be crossed. Much of the drug crime that marked New Orleans as the nation's murder capital in the 1980s and 1990s was concentrated in the projects that lie just above Rampart: unwitting tourists who expected the Quarter street party to continue as they blithely headed across the road were prime targets for muggings, or worse.

Today, most tourists will at least encounter Rampart Street at some time during their stay. Though it can still feel a little iffy at night, the presence of a couple of popular clubs and a handful of hotels have helped matters considerably, and many people wander freely here after dark with no problem.

▲ LOUIS ARMSTRONG PARK

Louis Armstrong Park and Congo Square

The impressive entrance to Louis Armstrong Park, a huge twinkling arch clearly visible the length of St Ann Street, promises more than the park itself delivers. Things may improve when the planned Jazz National

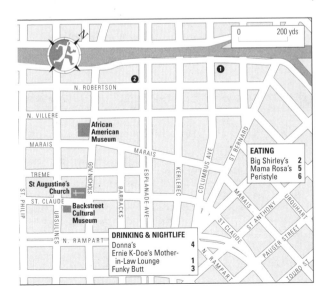

EATING

Big Shirley's	2
Mama Rosa's	5
Peristyle	6

DRINKING & NIGHTLIFE

Donna's	4
Ernie K-Doe's Mother-in-Law Lounge	1
Funky Butt	3

▲ SATCHMO STATUE, LOUIS ARMSTRONG PARK

Historical Park (see p.62) – including performance space and a visitor center – comes to fruition, but as yet it is a dreary place. The park is liveliest, and safest, during its occasional weekend music festivals, many of which are held in Congo Square, the small paved area to the left of the entrance arch.

In colonial times Congo Square was the Place des Nègres, where every Sunday slaves taken from all over West Africa would meet in their thousands to trade, perform religious rituals, make music and dance the *bamboula*, named after the large drums that beat the rhythm. At 9pm sharp a policeman would fire a cannon to signal the end of the proceedings – the penalty for breaking the curfew was twenty lashes. In the American era, the gatherings quickly became tourist attractions, thronging with vendors and sideshows, from which fascinated white visitors would return with shocked tales of weird voodoo rituals and depravity.

In 1994, a group of Mardi Gras Indians and Native Americans blessed Congo Square as sacred ground, and three years later it was placed on the National Register of Historic Places.

Our Lady of Guadalupe

411 N Rampart St at Conti. Our Lady of Guadalupe was built following a yellow-fever

Second Line parades

In the 1890s, the blacks of Tremé began to form benevolent – or mutual aid – societies, paying dues to cover funeral- and health-related expenses. Known as Social Aid and Pleasure Clubs, these societies also staged street parades, their members dancing and high-stepping – "Second Lining" – behind noisy brass bands. Nowadays, every fall, clubs with names like the Jolly Bunch, the Black Men of Labor, or the Sidewalk Steppers, strut through the streets in flamboyant matching shoes, hats, and umbrellas, to jubilant brass band music, gathering hundreds of spectators, and dancers ("the Second Line"), with them as they go. Though these are primarily neighborhood events, anyone is welcome to come along, and joining a Second Line is a highlight of any trip – an extraordinary, life-affirming experience that epitomizes so much of what makes the city, and Tremé, unique. Schedules are listed on ⓦwww.backstreetculturalmuseum.org; you can pick up flyers detailing routes a couple of weeks in advance at the museum itself (see p.116).

epidemic in 1826 as a Catholic mortuary chapel for the neighboring St Louis No. 1 cemetery. In those days both were outside the city limits, protecting the population from what were believed to be poisonous miasmas that emanated from the mountains of corpses and from the back-to-back funeral processions. A host of colorful shrines inside the church includes one to St Jude, patron saint of lost causes, piled high with hopefully placed novenas.

Set into a niche in the front wall, to the right as you enter the church, the colorful statue of the unknown "St Expedite," mysteriously delivered here, so the legend goes, in a crate simply stamped "expedite", is said to be worshipped by the city's voodooists.

St Louis No. 1

400 Basin St between Conti and St Louis. Mon–Sat 9am–3pm, Sun 9am–noon. Free. St Louis No. 1, one of New Orleans' distinctive European-style above-ground cemeteries, or "cities of the dead," is the oldest cemetery in the Mississippi valley. It was built in 1789, outside the city limits in an attempt to protect the population from the fatal fumes it believed emanated from corpses, and its tombs vary from early Spanish structures made of brick and plaster to later mausolea designed by eminent architects, including Benjamin Latrobe and J.N.B. de Pouilly.

On the fringe of the French Quarter, the cemetery is not safe to tour alone. It's a regular stop on the bus- and walking-tour circuit, however, and there is invariably a huddle of people by the simple tomb of "voodoo queen" Marie Laveau (see p.88), graffitied with countless brick-dust crosses. They're usually being told some tall tale about how, if you knock on the slab three times and mark a cross on her tomb, her spirit will grant you any favor. The family who own it have asked that this bogus, destructive tradition should stop, not least because people are taking chunks of brick from other tombs to make the crosses. Voodoo practitioners – responsible for the candles, plastic flowers, beads, and rum

▼ ST LOUIS NO. 1

bottles surrounding the plot – deplore the practice, too, regarding it as a desecration. Nearby, the enormous circular white marble structure, topped by a cross and angel, is the 1857 Italian Benevolent Society mausoleum, which has space for thousands of remains.

St Louis' other famous dead include Homer Plessy, whose refusal in 1892 to move from the whites-only section of a train led to the historic *Plessy* vs *Ferguson* case. His defeat gave rise to the Supreme Court's "separate but equal" ruling, which effectively established segregation in the South for another sixty years.

St Louis No. 2

200 N Claiborne Ave between Iberville and St Louis. Mon–Sat 9am–3pm, Sun 9am–noon. Free. Hemmed in between Tremé's Iberville housing project and the interstate, St Louis No. 2 is one of the most desolate, and dangerous, of the cities of the dead, and you should only venture here on a guided tour. Built in 1823, it's a prime example of local cemetery design, with a dead-straight center aisle, and many grandiose Greek Revival mausolea. A second Marie Laveau, believed to be the famed voodoo queen's daughter, has a tomb here – daubed with red-chalk crosses, like the original in St Louis No. 1 – as do swashbuckler Dominique You and his friend Mayor Nicholas Girod, who plotted together to return Napoleon from exile (see p.69).

Backstreet Cultural Museum

1116 St Claude at Ursulines. Tues–Sat 10am–5pm. $5. Walking around the fascinating Backstreet Cultural Museum, you feel as though you've been invited into someone's home and allowed to rummage through their personal possessions. Curator and guide Sylvester Francis has spent the last twenty years documenting and preserving local black street culture. Much of the collection revolves around urban mourning

The Jazz Funeral

Emerging in the late 1800s, organized by black benevolent societies for their members, "funerals with music" were led by brass bands who, after playing a dirge on the route from church to graveyard would then burst into a joyful tune to celebrate the prospect of eternal life. They were followed by mourners and then a Second Line who danced and exulted with the music.

By the 1970s many older brass band players had died, with few young musicians emerging to take their place. Distressed by this, local banjoist-composer Danny Barker began to teach aspiring youngsters not only to play the music but also to honor the spirit of the old marching bands. Slowly the music revived, and, in the 1980s, parading came back in force.

Very soon, however, local drug wars became so savage that the famed jazz funerals degenerated into highly charged, often violent, crack funerals. Now young, hip brass bands like ReBirth and the Soul Rebels were playing furious, fast-paced music at the funerals of their peers, while the Second Line would go as far as spraying beer over the coffin, wielding guns, and throwing bottles.

Nowadays, a variety of jazz funerals are held for local musicians, Mardi Gras Indians, and even Second Liners. As at any funeral, of course, tourists are not welcome.

customs, often to very moving effect: among the church programs, news clippings, and scrapbooks is a case of T-shirts, or "memory shirts," screenprinted with blurred photos of recently deceased loved ones – many of them young men, shot dead – and inscribed with dates of the victim's "Sunrise" and "Sunset." Also on show are frilly Second Line umbrellas and natty marching regalia, and a room of stunning, hand-sewn Mardi Gras Indian suits, emblazoned with feathers and sequins. For more on the Mardi Gras Indians, see p.166.

St Augustine's Church

1210 Gov Nicholls at St Claude. The oldest mixed-race church in the USA, the imposing Catholic St Augustine's has been active since 1842. It was designed by J.N.B. de Pouilly – who eight years later went on to remodel St Louis Cathedral in the French Quarter – and built with contributions from local blacks, freed and enslaved. Anyone is welcome to attend services; the church is fullest on the occasional Sundays when a guest singer or musician joins the choir for mass and the pews are packed with tourists. Its spruce interior, lined with tall white columns and illuminated by stained-glass porthole windows portraying French saints, also features bright, jazzy paintings and flags fluttering from the ceiling printed with affirmations – Purpose, Unity, Creativity – in English and Swahili.

African-American Museum

1418 Gov Nicholls at Villere ☎504/529-2976. Open by appointment. $5. The New Orleans African-American Museum is spread across three properties

set in flower-filled courtyards. The bulk of the collection is in the 1828 Meilleur House, a Caribbean-style plantation home, whose airy, high ceilinged-rooms make a great space for rotating exhibitions of art from Africa and the diaspora. Works by local black artists, from ceramics to textiles to photography, are displayed in a smaller, double-shotgun cottage and a three-room single shotgun on the grounds.

Restaurants

Big Shirley's

1500 Esplanade at N Robertson ☎504/301-9704; closed Mon. There's something for most people in this neighborhood restaurant, from Kermit's Swinging BBQ platter (dedicated to local jazz trumpeter Kermit Ruffins), with its ribs, chicken, shrimp, potato salad, vegetables, and fries, through soul food staples and gumbo to healthy vegetable specials. The friendly staff may well tease you if you don't finish your plate.

Mama Rosa's

616 N Rampart St at Toulouse ☎504/523-5546. Local favorite just a stone's throw away from the Quarter. The surroundings, service, and decor are plain, but the soft-crust pizzas are anything but: fresh, hot, and topped with a mess of good ingredients. Plus muffulettas, salads, and a great spaghetti with meatballs.

Peristyle

1041 Dumaine St at N Rampart ☎504/593-9535. Dinner only, closed Sun & Mon. Incongruously set on Rampart Street, this elegant, congenial bistro – *very* New Orleans, all dark wood,

▲ PERISTYLE

Live music

Donna's

800 N Rampart St at St Ann ☎504
/596-6914, @www.donnasbarandgrill
.com. Closed Tues & Wed. Run by
a husband-and-wife team, this
is a ramshackle locals' place that
attracts a big out-of-town crowd.
With a roster of brass band,
Mardi Gras Indian, and traditional
jazz acts, it's an absolute must-
see, and on Monday night it's
the *only* place to be. That's when
old-timer Bob French runs the
show, drumming with a who's
who of local stars – and some
audience members – who pop in
after their own gigs to check out
the scene. These are some of the
finest jam sessions you're likely
to hear, in a wonderful old-style
jazz house-party atmosphere. The
food – ribs, chicken, red beans,
and rice – is tasty, too, and the
prices low; on Monday you get
free barbecued chicken in the
break between sets. Cover varies;
one drink minimum.

checker-tiled floors, and
mismatched mirrors – is one of
the best places in town to eat
contemporary French-Creole-
New American cuisine. The
menu varies, but might include
pastis-poached oysters with
sturgeon caviar or pheasant
and artichoke ravioli, with
entrées (around $25) such as
poussin marinated in red wine
with herbed basmati rice.
Reservations essential; come
early and have a drink in the
lovely old bar.

▼ KERMIT RUFFINS JAMMING WITH BOB FRENCH AT DONNA'S

Ernie K-Doe's Mother-in-Law Lounge

1500 N Claiborne Ave at Columbus ☏504/947-1078, ⊛www.k-doe.com. Since the death of eccentric local R&B legend Ernie in 2001, his equally extraordinary wife Antoinette has kept their Tremé lounge (basically their living room, with the addition of a bar and a small stage) open as something of a shrine to the self-styled "Emperor of the World," complete with Ernie mannequins and commemorative pillows. Whether you hit a poetry night or an old school New Orleans R&B show, or simply end up spending the afternoon plugging quarters into the jukebox (featuring Ernie and New Orleans classics), you'll feel like you're in a movie. Hop in a cab and join the combination of supercool hipsters and unimpressed locals that make this place unique. Occasional cover if there's a show.

Funky Butt

714 N Rampart St at Orleans ☏504/558-0872, ⊛www.funkybutt .com. Intimate club named for an early haunt of jazz legend Buddy Bolden. The eclectic decor resembles an Art Deco bordello-cum-speakeasy-cum-Seventies pad, while the music – cool jazz, piano, funk, brass, and R&B – is great. Watch out particularly for the Wild Magnolias Mardi Gras Indians, Big Sam's Funky Nation, a funk-R&B brass band fronted by the Dirty Dozen's ebullient trombonist Big Sam, and the

Stooges, one of the very best of the new-style young brass bands. Cover varies.

Performing arts

Mahalia Jackson Theater of the Performing Arts

Louis Armstrong Park, Rampart St at St Ann ☏504/529-3000. A large, lavish setting for touring musicals, classical concerts, opera, and ballet, ice spectaculars, boxing, and so on.

Municipal Auditorium

1201 St Peter St, Louis Armstrong Park ☏504/565-7470. Built·in the 1930s, this is another large (5000-seat) venue for touring companies, sporting events, and big concerts.

▼ ERNIE – EMPEROR OF THE WORLD

The CBD

Neither as visually stunning nor as immediately appealing as the neighboring French Quarter, New Orleans' Central Business District (or **CBD**) is primarily of interest to visitors for its hotels and restaurants. Historically, however, its significance can't be overstressed: this was where American New Orleans started, created by vigorous Anglo newcomers who, after the Louisiana Purchase in 1803, built a new suburb of exchanges, insurance companies, banks, and shops – along with grand theaters and hotels – as they set about making themselves rich. New Orleans' center of commerce soon shifted from the French Quarter to this "American sector," or Faubourg St Mary, and in 1836 the city was carved into municipalities, each with its own council – a state of affairs which lasted until 1852. Canal Street was the dividing line between the first (Creole) and second (American) municipalities, and took over from Royal Street as the city's chief commercial thoroughfare.

▼ CANAL STREET

Canal Street

The widest main street (170ft) in America, and on the parade route for all the super krewes at Mardi Gras (see p.162), the once glorious Canal Street, which runs from the river to Lake Pontchartrain, is still the backbone of the city, dividing downtown (downriver) from uptown (upriver). There never was a canal here; the street started as a rough ditch cut along the ramparts of the city, separating it from the plantations – and later the American suburb – beyond. It was eventually filled to become the town commons, and as the Faubourg St Mary grew, settlers built homes along its muddy expanse. By the 1850s, all the homes had been replaced by department stores and opulent theaters. Though these are slowly disappearing, the gorgeous storefronts, decorated

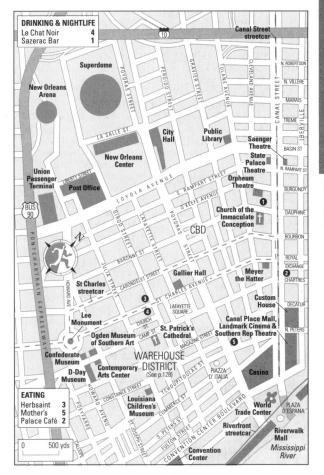

DRINKING & NIGHTLIFE

| Le Chat Noir | 4 |
| Sazerac Bar | 1 |

EATING

Herbsaint	3
Mother's	5
Palace Café	2

in Beaux Arts, Italianate, and Art Deco styles, for the most part remain, safe from the demolition that richer cities would have inflicted upon them. And it is still a lively shopping street, the handsome buildings filled with hotels, tacky souvenir stores, fast-food joints, and none-too-reputable electrical shops, with a jaunty new streetcar trundling up to Mid-City.

The Custom House

423 Canal St at Decatur. Mon–Fri 8am–4.30pm. Free. Along with the Mint (see p.62), the gray granite Custom House was a key player in New Orleans' grand antebellum building program. In order to handle the huge volume of commerce coming through the port, and to celebrate its value to the city, work started in 1848 on what was to be the largest

federal building in the nation; rooting such a monster in the city's shifting, soggy soil proved difficult, however, and the Custom House was only completed in 1881.

Mark Twain may have dismissed the foreboding classical exterior as "inferior to a gasometer," but fans of Greek Revival architecture should head inside, where, on the second floor, a huge marble hall, illuminated by a 54-foot skylight, recalls the lofty aspirations and optimism of the city's antebellum era. Flanked by fourteen fat Corinthian columns of Italian marble, the room is brimful of images of wealth and success: the capitals feature heads of Mercury, the Greek god of commerce, and Luna, goddess of the moon (playing on New Orleans' status as the Crescent City), while bas-relief panels depict proud portraits of Andrew Jackson and Bienville, founder of New Orleans.

Piazza d'Italia

This surreal jumble of Classic-style columns, arches, and relief facades, fashioned in marble, steel, and neon, was built in 1978 by Charles Moore as a tribute to the city's Italian community. Having won a number of awards for its cutting-edge Postmodern design, the piazza fell into disrepair in the 1980s, becoming a fly-blown wasteland best avoided. Today, spruced up by the swanky new *Loew's* hotel next door, it's a dynamic, colorful space once more, with a huge, staggered fountain that makes a great playground for kids on hot afternoons.

▼ PIAZZA D'ITALIA

Church of the Immaculate Conception

130 Baronne St at Canal. The decorative interior of this oddly Moorish Jesuit church incorporates huge arches and dazzling stained glass with fine cast-iron spiral columns and pews. Designed by local architect James Freret, the gilded bronze altar, with its trio of onion domes, won first prize at the Paris Exposition of 1867. Like so many of New Orleans' buildings, the original church, built in 1851, threatened to collapse under its own weight into the swampy earth; what you see today – a perfect replica – dates from 1930.

Lafayette Square

Laid out in 1788, Lafayette Square was the political hub of the American sector, an

▲ CHURCH OF THE IMMACULATE CONCEPTION

Anglo version of the Creole Place d'Armes (today's Jackson Square). Today, surrounded by dreary court buildings and offices, it's the venue for regular outdoor concerts featuring big-name local and regional bands. On the lakeside of the square stands a bronze statue of John McDonogh, outspoken abolitionist and leading light in the American Colonization Society, which advocated the return of slaves to Africa. Upon his death in 1850, he left his considerable riches for the establishment of racially mixed public schools; many of New Orleans' public schools are the result of that legacy. The statue, designed in 1898 at a cost of $7000, was funded by nickel donations from the city's schoolchildren.

Gallier Hall

545 St Charles Ave at Lafayette. The grandest example of Greek Revival architecture in New Orleans, magnificent Gallier Hall is fronted by an ornate ninety-foot facade with ten fluted white Ionic columns and a pediment featuring Justice, Liberty, and Commerce. It was designed by James Gallier Sr as the City Hall for the second municipality; by the time it was dedicated in 1853, however, New Orleans had reunited, and the building served as seat of government for the whole city right up to the 1950s. These days, Gallier Hall is the site of one of the premier Mardi Gras parade-viewing platforms, packed with assorted bigwigs, including the mayor. The enormous floats stop here for quite a while, and experienced bead-beggars know to stake out the spot across the street. For more on Mardi Gras, see p.162.

St Patrick's Church

710 Camp St at Girod. James Gallier Sr, though best known for his accomplished Greek Revival buildings, also had a hand in the Neo-Gothic St Patrick's Church, near Lafayette Square. In 1838 Irish architects Charles and James Dakin set to work on rebuilding the small wooden church that had stood on this site since 1833 – the second municipality was thriving, and needed a Catholic place of worship to equal St Louis Cathedral, where services were held only in French. Work was completed by Gallier, who designed the interior with its fine stained glass, elaborate altar, and sweeping vaulting.

Shops

Canal Place Mall

333 Canal St at N Peters ☎504/522-9200. A tranquil place to shop, with upmarket national chains like Williams-Sonoma, Pottery Barn, Saks Fifth Avenue, Jaeger, Gucci, and Betsey Johnson, plus local stores RHINO and the shop of New Orleans jewelry designer Mignon Faget. It also features a four-screen

independent cinema (see p.196) and a rep theater (p.126).

Meyer the Hatter

120 St Charles Ave at Canal ☎1-800/882-4287. Closed Sun. "Over 100 years of hats" at this traditional store. Most of the space is taken up by Biltmores – the New Orleans jazzman's favorite – but you'll also find Stetsons, baseball caps, Kangols, and much more.

Rapp's Luggage

604 Canal St at St Charles ☎504/568-1953. Closed Sun. The most reputable baggage store on Canal Street, with a good, reasonably priced selection including Samsonite, Tumi, Timberland, and Jans backpacks, along with briefcases and purses, as well as a repair service.

▲ MEYER THE HATTER

Restaurants

Herbsaint

701 St Charles Ave at Girod ☎504/524-4114, ⊕www.herbsaint .com. Lunch only Sat, closed Sun. Effortlessly stylish, relaxed bistro offering affordable French-influenced food. It's especially good at lunchtime, when people come to enjoy themselves rather than to grab a hurried business lunch, and the streetcar rumbles past the huge windows. The food is simple and fresh – classics include antipasto and fried frogs' legs with herbs, while concoctions like crabmeat salad with yellow beets and avocado, or the decadent chocolate beignets, have a more contemporary spin.

Mother's

401 Poydras St at Tchoupitoulas ☎504/523-9656. Though tourists go into a tizzy about *Mother's*,

thrilled to be eating N'Awlins home cooking in a downhome ambience (brick walls, concrete floors, brusque counter service), locals complain that it's become too pricey. That said, the portions are big, and the food is good, especially if you go for breakfast – black ham (the sweet, crunchy skin of a baked ham) is a favorite, dished up with buttery biscuits and grits – or one of their overstuffed po-boys. No credit cards.

Palace Café

605 Canal St at Chartres ☎504/523-1661. Lovely, casually elegant restaurant in a grand old music-store building on the edge of the Quarter. Always buzzing, with the ambience of a nineteenth-century European café, it's big and airy, with marble tables, check-tiled floors, a spiral staircase sweeping up to a mezzanine and sunny walls lined

with vintage French posters. The food, contemporary Creole, is first-rate, from the fragrant oyster pan roast to the potato pie mashed with pork debris, spinach, melted cheese, and gravy. The jazz brunch is lovely, with three delicious courses from $18, and a trio of strolling musicians who play requests.

Bars

Sazerac Bar

Fairmont Hotel, 123 Baronne St at Canal ☎504/529-4733. Historic Art Deco bar in a grand old hotel. With its original oak fittings and colorful "Caribbean-Cubist" murals by Paul Ninas, it attracts a well-dressed local and business traveler clientele – a very different scene from the shabby French Quarter bars, but just as much part of the New Orleans landscape. The Sazerac cocktail (see p.196) was invented here, and most people order one.

Performing arts

Le Chat Noir

715 St Charles Ave at Girod ☎504 /581-5812, ☞www.cabaretlechatnoir .com. This upscale 1940s-style supper club venue features cabaret, musical revues, dance, traditional jazz, piano, stand-up comedy, and alternative theater. No jeans or shorts.

New Orleans Arena

1501 Girod St, ☞www .neworleansarena.com. Tagging alongside the Superdome like a clingy kid brother, the New Orleans Arena hosts sports events and big-name music acts.

Orpheum Theater

129 University Place at Canal ☎504/524-3285, ☞www .orpheumneworleans.com. Historic venue, built in 1921 as a vaudeville theater and movie house. Today, oozing faded grandeur, it makes an ideal base

▼ JAZZ BRUNCH AT THE PALACE CAFÉ

for the Louisiana Philharmonic Orchestra.

Saenger Theatre

143 N Rampart St at Canal ☎504/524-2490, ⊛www.saengertheatre.com. Beautifully restored 1920s movie theater, replete with classical statuary, glittering chandeliers, and a star-spangled night-sky ceiling. It's a lovely venue for touring Broadway productions, big-name soul and blues concerts, and classic movies.

Southern Rep Theater

Canal Place, 333 Canal St ☎504/522.6545, ⊛www.southernrep .com. Intimate venue in this conveniently situated mall (see p.123) featuring the work of Southern playwrights – up-and-coming and established – performed by local actors.

State Palace Theater

1108 Canal St at N Rampart ☎504/522-4435, ⊛www.statepalace.com. Gorgeous old theater, built as a vaudeville house in the 1920s. Today, it is a regular venue for rock, rap, ska, and R&B concerts, as well as the occasional movie show.

Superdome

Sugar Bowl Drive ☎504/587-3633, ⊛www.superdome.com. At 52 acres, 27 stories high and with a diameter of 680ft, the Superdome is one of the largest buildings in the world. Completed in 1975 at a cost of nearly $200 million, this gargantuan stadium is variously used for Saints' football games, teeming trade shows, major rock concerts, and more Super Bowl games than have been held in any other city.

The Warehouse District

Officially part of the CBD, **the Warehouse District**, or Arts District, is an up-and-coming area of low-rent studios, galleries, and loft apartments, loosely bounded by Julia Street, the Expressway, Convention Center Boulevard, and St Charles Avenue. During the antebellum era, vast depots stood here, storing goods ready to be loaded onto ocean-going ships and waiting to be transported upriver by steamboat. After Reconstruction, however, the district deteriorated into a no-go zone, only reviving a century later when chosen as the site of the 1984 World's Fair, which brought visibility to the area's previously neglected lofts and factory buildings. Today, though the district features a couple of the city's major museums and galleries, along with some good restaurants, bars, and clubs, it is not a great place to walk around at night.

Julia Street architecture

Although many structures were demolished in the 1960s and 70s, a profusion of the Warehouse District's original buildings – churches, factories, and tall brick townhouses, as well as warehouses – remains, offering a counterpoint to the Creole flavor of the Quarter. Here, Federal, Neoclassical and Greek Revival styles dominate, reflecting the very American nature of the antebellum Faubourg St Mary. At 545 Julia Street you'll see three of the district's earliest warehouses – simple, shuttered structures built in 1833; compare these with the larger, utilitarian building at no. 329, New Orleans' first reinforced concrete construction. In the 600 block between St Charles and Camp stands a parade of spruce, renovated row houses known as the Thirteen Sisters. When they were built in 1833, these red-brick residences were the most desirable in the American sector, modeled in the Federal style favored in the northeastern states;

just sixty years later they had declined into slums. Today they're alive again, filled with galleries and antique stores, architects' offices, and a wonderfully old-time corner grocery.

Arts District galleries

When people talk about the Arts District they're mainly referring to Julia Street, which has a growing reputation for showcasing the best in regional and national contemporary art. While hopping between the hip, very expensive, private galleries along here – easily done on foot – is worth an afternoon, note that many of them close for summer, and some shut up shop during the day on reception days; consult the listings papers *Lagniappe* or *Gambit* (see p.189) before setting off. Probably the best time to visit is on the first Saturday of every month from October to May, when the string of art openings pulls a mixed crowd of uptowners, art students, and conventioneers, all nibbling cheese, sipping Chablis,

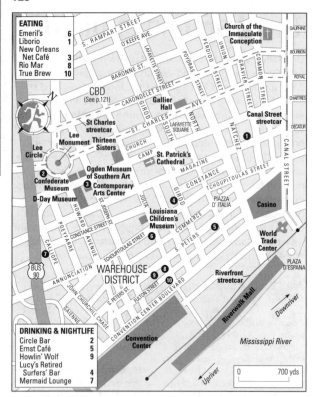

EATING

Emeril's	6
Liborio	1
New Orleans Net Café	3
Rio Mar	8
True Brew	10

DRINKING & NIGHTLIFE

Circle Bar	2
Ernst Café	5
Howlin' Wolf	9
Lucy's Retired Surfers' Bar	4
Mermaid Lounge	7

and checking out the art and each other.

The biggest shindig of all, the place for the local art world to see and be seen, is Art for Art's Sake (see p.194), held on the first Saturday in October. The blocks around Julia and Camp streets are closed off to create a street party with live music and drinks stalls; a shuttle bus runs to and from the galleries on Magazine Street, and later the revels shift to the Contemporary Arts Center (see p.131). Jammin' on Julia, on the first Saturday in May, and White Linen Night, in August, are similar, though smaller-scale events.

Louisiana Children's Museum

420 Julia St at Constance. Tues–Sat 9.30am–4.30pm, Sun noon–4.30pm. $6. In a sturdy 1861 warehouse topped by an elaborate cornice, the Louisiana Children's Museum is worth a trip if you've got bored kids in tow. While on any given day you can bet some of the exhibits don't work, and others are wearyingly earnest, there are enough things to wind up, push, pull, and plunge to keep younger ones diverted for an hour or so. And few people – kids or adults – will be able to resist seeing themselves on screen as a news anchor or weatherperson in the KidWatch TV studio.

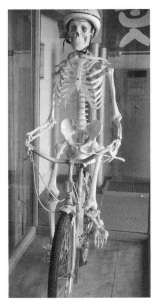

▲ LOUISIANA CHILDREN'S MUSEUM

Confederate Museum

929 Camp St at Lee Circle. Mon–Sat 10am–4pm. $5. Anyone who needs reminding that easy-living New Orleans has its roots entrenched in the Deep South should take a trip to the Confederate Museum. A gloomy Romanesque Revival hulk, purpose-designed by Thomas Sully in 1891 as a place for Confederate veterans to display their mementos, this self-styled "Battle Abbey of the South" is a relic from a bygone age. Confederate President Jefferson Davis, who died in New Orleans in 1889, lay in state here briefly, and there remains a funereal air about the place, with its bittersweet remembrances of long-lost generals and their forgotten families. Its aim remains to tell "the story of insult and oppression . . . pillage and ruin . . . want and suffering and humiliation and insult and punishment."

Inside the church-like hall, glass cases are filled with flags, swords, mess-kits, uniforms, and helmets. There are wordy accounts of battles and generals, but very little background detail – when the museum was built the "lost cause" would have been fresh in visitors' minds – and certainly no attempt at hindsight or analysis. That said, the place has an undeniable pull. Along with affecting sepia photos, oddities include a crown of thorns hand-woven by Pope Pius IX and sent to Davis as an encouraging gift. There's also an account of the Confederate Native Guards, free blacks who signed up but weren't allowed to fight by the other Confederate states, and on Union Major Benjamin "Beast" Butler, who commanded the military rule of the city after it fell to Union troops in 1862. So unpopular was the Beast with diehard Rebels – he hanged a man for tearing down the Union flag, for example – that local beauties would retch loudly as any Union soldier walked by. In a fit of pique at the behavior of what he called "these she-adders," Butler announced General Order 28, claiming "When any female shall by word, gesture, or movement, insult or show contempt for any officer of the United States, she shall be regarded and held liable to be treated as a woman of the town plying her vocation." The order was soon recalled, as was Butler himself in December 1862.

The Confederate Museum is just a stone's throw from Lee Circle, which centers on a bronze statue of the Confederate general atop an 1884 sixty-foot marble column. The statue faces north, of course.

Ogden Museum of Southern Art

925 Camp St at St Joseph @www
.ogdenmuseum.org. Tues, Wed &
Fri–Sun 9.30am–5.30pm, Thurs
9.30am–8.30pm. $10. Occupying
a swanky four-story gallery, the
Ogden Museum of Southern
Art runs the gamut from rare
eighteenth-century watercolors
through self-taught art to
contemporary sculpture. While
many of the artists are lesser
known, it's a compelling place,
evoking a strong sense of this
distinctive region so preoccupied
with notions of the land, of
family and religion, poverty
and the past, violence and loss.
The photography selecton is
particularly strong, with E.J.
Bellocq's direct and humane
portraits of Storyville prostitutes,
Clarence John Laughlin's
haunting 1930s evocations of a
devastated, ghost-ridden South,
and some fine hyper-realist work
from Eudora Welty. Elsewhere,

▼ OGDEN MUSEUM

highlights include folk art
by Clementine Hunter, the
African-American artist whose
colorful paintings and quilts
recall her plantation childhood
in northern Louisiana, and 1960s
jazz portraits by painter Noel
Rockmore.

National D-Day Museum

945 Magazine St at Howard. Daily
9am–5pm. $10. Shaped by the
vision of the late New Orleans-
based historian Stephen E.
Ambrose, the massive, always
crowded National D-Day
Museum opened on June 6,
2000, the 56th anniversary of
the Allied invasion of Europe.
The museum's core collection
concentrates on the events
of that dramatic day, but
emphasizes that the Normandy
invasion was not the only D-
Day in history. Considering any
shoreline assault to be a D-Day
(D simply stands for "Day"),
the museum offers displays
that range across the endless
island-hopping of the Pacific
War, too, thus tracing the entire
US involvement of World War
II. For all but diehard military
buffs, the sheer quantity of
the museum's hardware and
uniforms may prove exhausting,
but luckily there is enough film
footage, background material,
and, especially, oral testimony
from both sides of the conflict
to broaden the focus.

In theory, visits begin with
one of two 50-minute film
shows, but you may as well head
straight upstairs to the galleries.
On the third floor, "Before
the War" and "The Road to
War" lead into a thorough
exposition of the Normandy
invasion. Oral testimonies
juxtapose the experiences of
the 1.5 million GIs who were
stationed in Britain prior to

District, it's a beautifully designed space, and there's always something interesting going on, from the temporary shows on the ground floor to major exhibitions upstairs, with a lively program of cutting-edge performances, movies, lectures, and workshops. It also hosts October's Art for Art's Sake bash (see p.194).

Shops and markets

Crescent City Farmers Market

700 Magazine St at Girod ☎504/861-5898. Sat 8am–noon. Stalls selling fresh herbs, fruit and vegetables, breads, cheese, cut meats, and organic wines. They also have coffee and pastry stands, live music, and celebrity chef demonstrations.

▲ NATIONAL D-DAY MUSEUM

the landings with those of the nervous German defenders of the Atlantic Wall, a network of fortifications that extended along Europe's northwestern seaboard. Eisenhower's nerve-wracking decision to launch "Operation Overlord" on June 6, 1944, is chronicled in detail through timelines, photographs, and documents.

The Contemporary Arts Center

900 Camp St at St Joseph ☺www .cacno.org. Tues–Sun 11am–5pm. Ground-floor galleries free; changing exhibitions $5. Housed in a restored nineteenth-century warehouse and ice-cream factory, the Contemporary Arts Center (CAC) is the city's premier modern art gallery. A kind of anchor for the Arts

Cafés

New Orleans Net Café

900 Camp St at St Joseph ☎504/523-0990. Internet access is free (30min maximum) at this café, linked to the CAC – and they serve espresso, tea, wine, sandwiches, and pastries to boot.

True Brew

200 Julia St at Fulton ☎504/524-8441, for theater info 524-8440. Closed Thurs. Comfortable coffeehouse that serves good espresso, healthy breakfasts, wraps, soups, salads, and quiches in a relaxed atmosphere. Also doubles as a theater, putting on short dramas and comedies of local interest, along with stand-up and open-mic events.

Restaurants

Emeril's

800 Tchoupitoulas St at Julia
☎504/528-9393, ⊛www.emerils
.com/restaurants/emerils. Closed lunch
Sat & Sun. Celebrity chef Emeril
Lagasse's flagship restaurant is
a noisy, flashy place, filled with
delighted tourists and special-
occasion locals enthusing over
the decorative, complicated
Creole cuisine. Entrées ($20–35)
include double-cut pork chop
with green chile mole sauce,
or duck confit with kiln-dried
berries, Stilton, arugula, and
vanilla vinaigrette. For dessert
most people go for the bus-
sized banana cream pie. It's
pricey, but Lagasse fans will love
it. Reservations essential.

Liborio

321 Magazine St at Gravier ☎504/581-
9680. Sat dinner only, closed Sun. This
family-run lunchtime favorite
is also good for inexpensive
dinners: traditional Cuban dishes
include slow-roasted lemon-
marinated lamb, home-made
tamales, and *ropa vieja* ("old
clothes") – shredded beef in
garlicky tomato sauce with
brown rice, black beans, and
plantains – while the *medianoche*,
sweet bread stuffed with ham,
cheese, pork, and pickles, is an
interesting variation on the
classic Cuban sandwich.

Rio Mar

800 S Peters St at Julia ☎504/525-
3474. Closed Sun and lunch Sat. New
Orleans seafood meets Spanish
cuisine in this terrific restaurant.
To start, you can't go wrong
with the tuna empanadas or
daily special ceviches; proceed
with paella or fish-packed
zarzuela (stew) – $11 at lunch,
$19 dinner – and you'll be in
heaven.

Bars

Ernst Café

600 S Peters St at Lafayette
☎504/525-8544. Friendly local
joint – said to be a favorite of
honorary New Orleanian John
Goodman – that looks much
as it did when it opened in
1902, with pressed-tin walls and
a fine old wooden bar. Quiet
during the day, it fills in the
evening with an older, mellower
set of regulars than you'll find
in the other CBD after-work
haunts. Soak up the beer with

▼ EMERIL'S

blue-plate specials, gumbo, and po-boys, served in the bar or in a small dining room.

Lucy's Retired Surfers' Bar

701 Tchoupitoulas St at Girod ☎504/523-8995. Something of a twenty- and early thirtysomethings pick-up joint, this cheery bar is packed after office hours with a white-collar clientele. In an attempt to evoke a West Coast scene, the walls are lined with surfboards, beach movies flicker on the TVs, and chirpy bar staff dole out garish, frosted cocktails and decent Tex-Mex food.

Live music and clubs

Circle Bar

1032 St Charles Ave at Lee Circle ☎504/588-2616. This very hip bar, incongruously set in a crumbling house standing alone in the shadow of the Expressway, crams live bands into its tiny space most nights. With an inspired, eclectic booking policy, it's renowned for resurrecting jazz and R&B legends from obscurity, and always pulls a gorgeous, arty, hard-partying crowd. Happy hour Mon–Fri 4–8pm, Sat and Sun 5–8pm. Usually no cover.

Howlin' Wolf

828 S Peters St at Julia ☎504/522-WOLF, ⊛www.thehowlinwolf.com. Big, bare-bones club that attracts a mixed bunch of grungy young locals and tourists for alternative rock, funk, and R&B. Also occasional acoustic open-mic nights and classic/cult movies. Cover $5–15.

Mermaid Lounge

1100 Constance St at John Churchill Chase ☎504/524-4747, ⊛www.mermaidlounge.com. Hidden away down a dead-end alley, this tiny local bar, owned and managed by local musicians and artists, features a mixed bag of garage, punk, avant-garde music, klezmer, blues, funk, and Cajun (don't miss the ancient Hackberry Ramblers). There's also a flea market, on the third Sunday of every month, held in the courtyard (noon–5pm). Cover varies.

Performing arts

Contemporary Arts Center

900 Camp St at St Joseph ☎504/528-3800, ⊛www.cacno.org. Modern gallery and performance space hosting one-off art exhibitions, dance, performance art, video installations, avant-garde movies, and experimental theater.

PLACES The Warehouse District

▼ CIRCLE BAR

The Garden District

Shaded by jungles of subtropical foliage, the glorious houses of the Garden District evoke a nostalgic vision of the Deep South in a profusion of galleries, columns, and balconies. This grand residential district drapes itself seductively across an area just thirteen blocks wide and five deep, bounded by Magazine Street and St Charles, Jackson, and Louisiana avenues.

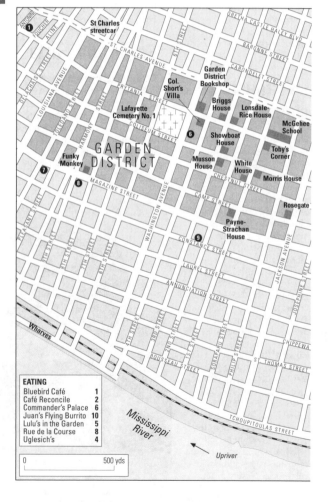

EATING

Bluebird Café	1
Café Reconcile	2
Commander's Palace	6
Juan's Flying Burrito	10
Lulu's in the Garden	5
Rue de la Course	8
Uglesich's	4

Around two miles upriver from the French Quarter, the Garden District started life in 1834 as the separate city of Lafayette. It was built by the energetic breed of Anglo-Americans who announced their ever-accumulating wealth by constructing sumptuous mansions in huge, lush gardens. Although the district now officially forms part of uptown New Orleans, it retains its own proud identity, with its august residences remaining in the hands of the monied elite. The Garden District is best explored on an official walking tour (see

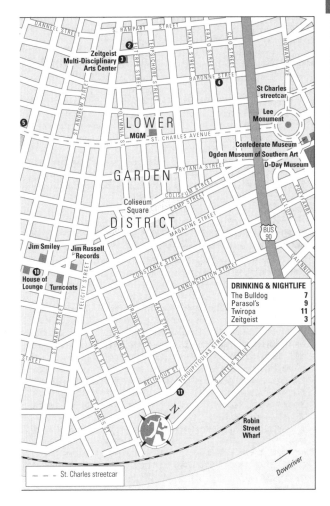

DRINKING & NIGHTLIFE

The Bulldog	7
Parasol's	9
Twiropa	11
Zeitgeist	3

- - - St. Charles streetcar

p.191) or one of the self-guided tours available from the tourist office (see p.188). The mansions themselves are only open to the public on special tours during New Orleans' five-day Spring Fiesta (☏504/581-1367).

St Charles Avenue

The development of the Garden District was accelerated by the arrival, in 1835, of the New Orleans and Carrollton Railroad, which ran along St Charles Avenue, the broad street bordering the suburb on its lakeside edge. After 1893, when the streetcar line was electrified, merchants flourishing in the post-Civil War South found that to live on "the avenue" was the ideal way to display their new wealth. Today, while lower St Charles Avenue is a scrappy ragbag of empty lots and architectural nonentities, once you reach the Garden District the private mansions cut as impressive a dash as they did a century ago, their cut-glass doors sparkling like priceless crystal. To see the best of them, continue on the streetcar and head uptown toward Audubon Park (see p.144).

Magazine Street

Running parallel to St Charles Avenue, and forming the riverside boundary of the Garden District, Magazine Street is the other main channel between Canal Street and uptown. A six-mile stretch of shotgun houses filled with thrift and antique stores, designer clothes shops, coffee bars, restaurants, and art galleries, this is one of the very best places to shop in the city, and is especially lively at the weekends. Sadly the streetcars do not pass this way; the #11 bus runs the length of the road, but services are sporadic.

The St Charles streetcar

There can be few more relaxing ways of passing an hour or so in New Orleans than planting yourself on a mahogany bench on the St Charles streetcar, catching the breeze from the open window, and watching as one of America's loveliest avenues unfolds in front of you.

The streetcar, now a National Historic Monument, began in 1835 as the New Orleans and Carrollton Railroad, a steam-powered train that took a day to cover the six and a half miles from Canal Street via Lafayette to the resort town of Carrollton. After the Civil War, the inefficient steam engines were replaced by mules – a cleaner, quieter form of transport – until overhead electricity was introduced in 1893.

The streetcar network spread quickly, with cars traveling three abreast along tracks crisscrossing Canal Street and the French Quarter. By the time Tennessee Williams was penning his 1947 play *A Streetcar Named Desire*, the service was already dwindling, faced with competition from motorbuses, and by 1964 only the St Charles line remained.

In the 1980s, a new streetcar line was introduced along a two-mile stretch of the riverfront, and in 2004 the old Canal Street line, which heads up via Carrollton Avenue to City Park, was reinstated. Neither, however, has the romantic, historic cachet of the sage green St Charles cars. For more on the practicalities of streetcar travel, see pp.189–90.

Garden District architecture

The mansions of the Garden District were built in a variety of architectural styles, according to the whim of each owner. The earliest homes stood one to a block, situated on the corners and fronted by brick flagstones that came over as ballast on ships returning from Europe. As fortunes were made, tastes became more and more flamboyant, each nouveau-riche planter and merchant trying to outdo his neighbor. Today you'll see ordered, columned Greek Revival structures, romantic Italianate villas, Moorish follies, Second Empire piles, and fanciful Queen Anne mansions, plus a number of buildings that defy categorization, with motifs mixed up together to form transitional, or hybrid, styles.

The Lower Garden District

The Lower Garden District is a loose term for the area between the Warehouse District and the Garden District proper. Sprawling down through a cluster of unpronounceable streets named after the Greek muses, via gentrifying Coliseum Square to the river, it's a hip, racially mixed neighborhood, the once decorative, now decaying, nineteenth-century buildings housing a motley population of artists and poor families. While it's no great shakes for sightseeing, it does have a couple of budget hotels, and lower Magazine Street is fantastic for shopping, with various alternative galleries, thrift stores, and places to eat. Below Jackson Avenue the street is peppered with desolate, run-down blocks, however, so keep your wits about you if you decide to walk it.

Toby's Corner

2340 Prytania St at First. The oldest surviving house in the Garden District, the Greek Revival mansion known as Toby's Corner was built in 1838, in unadorned plantation style, with a raised floor to prevent waterlogging. Thomas Toby himself, a Philadelphia native, had made a fortune by inventing a revolutionary cotton hauler, then promptly lost most of it backing the doomed Texan revolution of 1835.

The McGehee School

2434 Prytania St at First. Fronted by mighty Corinthian columns, the private McGehee School opposite Toby's Corner is housed in what was formerly the residence of Union sympathizer Bradish Johnson. Built during Reconstruction, the showy Second Empire trophy was the envy of every sugar planter in town, boasting not only an exquisite domed

▼ ST CHARLES STREETCAR

▲ ITALIANATE VILLA

marble staircase, but also a newfangled elevator, a sure sign of wealth and distinction.

Joseph Morris House and the White House

1331 First St at Coliseum/1312 First St at Coliseum. The lovely rose-pink Joseph Morris House is a quintessential example of the dreamy Italianate style that swept through the Garden District in the 1860s. Its romantic aspect, enhanced by a web of cast-iron galleries, is perfectly set off by the orderly, straight-down-the-line Greek Revival White House opposite.

Anne Rice's old house (Rosegate)

1239 First St at Chestnut. A gorgeous Italianate-Greek Revival hybrid, Rosegate was home to novelist Anne Rice between 1991 and 2004. This was also the fictional home of her Mayfair witches, and appears in her final vampire novel, *Blood Canticle*, written before she left her beloved New Orleans following the death of

her husband. Built in 1856, it was the first house on the block, and today its elaborate floriate iron fence encloses other, newer houses. Notice the Egyptian "keyhole" front door, flaring out at the base, and the gallery ceiling, painted sky-blue to trick insects from nesting there.

Payne-Strachan House

1134 First St at Camp. The columned, relatively unostentatious Payne-Strachan House is a prime specimen of antebellum Greek Revival styling. Built in 1849 for the pro-Union planter Jacob Payne, it is most notable for being where Jefferson Davis, president of the Confederacy, died in 1889, while visiting Payne's son-in-law. A granite slab outside commemorates the event.

Musson House

1331 Third St at Coliseum. The Italianate Musson House, a fanciful, pink-clapboard structure fronted with fabulous cast-iron balconies, was built in 1850 for Michel Musson, the Creole uncle of the French Impressionist painter Edgar Degas. After the Civil War, having lost much of his wealth, Musson abandoned the Anglo-dominated Garden District in favor of Esplanade Avenue, the Creole equivalent of St Charles Avenue.

Showboat House

1415 Third St at Coliseum. One of the Garden District's most palatial properties, the gallery-swathed Robinson Mansion, or Showboat House, is an Italianate-Greek Revival structure designed in 1859 by eminent architects Henry Howard and James Gallier Jr. It is best known, prosaically, for its early form of indoor plumbing, whereby the roof acted as a large vessel to collect rainwater that was then channeled down into the house.

▲ MUSSON HOUSE

Briggs House

2605 Prytania St at Third. The Garden District's only Neo-Gothic mansion, the stern-looking Briggs House, was designed by James Gallier Sr in 1847. Though there are a couple of significant Neo-Gothic buildings – also the work of Gallier – in the CBD, as a rule Southerners weren't that keen on the narrow windows and arches that characterized the style. This building, whose pared-down aspect does look a little out of place in the overblown Garden District, was built for an English insurance broker.

Colonel Short's Villa

1448 Fourth St at Prytania. Yet another Henry Howard structure, the Italianate Colonel Short's Villa was built for $25,000 in 1859 – a relatively paltry sum, even then. Just a few years later, it was commandeered by Yankee forces, who enjoyed its facilities

▼ ROSEGATE

▲ COLONEL SHORT'S VILLA

are sinking into the grunge below – as the soft red brick cracks and the marble tablets buckle, some of them are slowly opening, revealing the *caveau* within. Anne Rice has used this decaying cemetery as a location in many of her novels – in 1995, she even staged a mock jazz funeral here to launch publication of *Memnoch the Devil*; the "corpse" was herself, wearing an antique wedding dress, in an open coffin carried by pallbearers.

Though you're unlikely to face any real danger wandering around Lafayette cemetery alone, it's probably just as well to take a guided tour; see p.191 for details.

for the duration of the Civil War. While the building itself, with its columns and galleries, is undeniably striking, it's the cast-iron cornstalk fence that grabs your attention. A tangle of corn cobs and morning glories, it was picked, during the city's cast-iron craze, from the same catalog as its twin in the French Quarter (see p.81). You'll spot crumbly patches, where the fence is rusting away: cast iron, despite its decorative qualities, tends to be less durable than the simpler, hand-wrought iron favored in the early nineteenth century.

Lafayette No. 1 Cemetery

1400 Washington Ave between Prytania and Coliseum. Mon–Fri 7.30am–2.30pm, Sat 7.30am–noon. Free. Lafayette Cemetery, in the heart of the Garden District, was built in 1833 for Lafayette's wealthy, Anglo-American population. Its wide intersecting avenues are now swathed with overgrown foliage, and many of the tombs

Shops

Funky Monkey

3127 Magazine St at Ninth ☏504/899-5587. Fabulous designer costumes, vintage rags, wigs, bags, shoes, and make-up, with a very good choice of men's suits. It's just the place to throw together a unique costume or disguise.

Garden District Bookshop

The Rink, 2727 Prytania St at Washington ☏504//895-2266. Strong selection of local titles, fiction, travel guides, limited editions, and autographed copies, plus regular author signings and literary events.

House of Lounge

2044 Magazine St at Josephine ☏504/671-8300. This glamorous salon, a throwback to 1930s Hollywood, is a drop-dead gorgeous setting to splash out on vampish lingerie and boudoir attire, with a nice line in froufrou accessories and jewelry.

▲ FUNKY MONKEY

yourself out in costumes worn by the stars. Rental only, from $35 to $500 per day.

Turncoats

1926 Magazine St at St Mary
℡504/299-9004. Hip, creative, and alternative, this place typifies the vibrant Lower Magazine Street scene – it's an art gallery, clothing exchange, and vintage/customized/designer clothes store all rolled into one.

Cafés

Rue de la Course

3128 Magazine St at Ninth
℡504/899-0242. With their pressed-tin walls, café-au-lait decor, ceiling fans, and reading lamps, the *Rue* chain of coffeeshops exude an old-Europe ambience. Liveliest of the lot, this spacious Garden District branch is usually teeming with students poring over fat textbooks or playing Scrabble. The coffee, brewed with beans from around the world, is great – for a real indulgence, try the caffè crema – and there are plenty of biscotti, cakes, and bagels. There's another branch, in the Lower Garden District, at 1500 Magazine St (℡504/529-1455).

Jim Russell Records

1837 Magazine St at St Mary
℡504/522-2602. Large collection of rare vinyl, along with singles, cassettes, and CDs, specializing in soul, R&B, hip-hop, and blues. They ship worldwide.

MGM

1617 St Charles Ave at Terpsichore
℡504/581-3999. Closed Thurs & Sun. Hollywood's MGM studio was renowned for its big-budget extravaganzas – now you can kit

▼ RUE DE LA COURSE

Restaurants

Bluebird Café

3625 Prytania St at Foucher
☎504/895-7166. On the uptown fringes of the Garden District, this airy, inexpensive, vaguely hippyish hangout serves good, healthy home cooking for breakfast and lunch. Lines form outside, especially at the weekend, for the big all-day breakfasts, which include huevos rancheros, corned-beef hash, buckwheat pancakes, and "power" eggs (with tamari and yeast). They also do daily plate lunch specials, which you can wash down with virtuous herbal teas and fresh OJ. No reservations; no credit cards.

Café Reconcile

1631 Oretha Castle Haley Blvd at Felicity ☎504/568-1157. Breakfast and lunch only, closed Sat & Sun. Excellent non-profit venture, spearheaded by a Jesuit church, where local underprivileged teens are trained for jobs in the hospitality industry. The dining room is warm, friendly, and spotless, prices are ridiculously low, and the food is absolutely delicious: try a big Southern breakfast for $4 or a plate lunch of meatloaf, fried chicken, or white beans and shrimp with rice (around $5).

Commander's Palace

1403 Washington Ave at Coliseum
☎504/899-8221, ⊛www
.commanderspalace.com. The world-famous grande dame of the Garden District is set in a turquoise-and-white 1880s mansion with a maze of rooms and a tropical, oak-shaded courtyard. The heart-thumpingly rich Creole food deserves the hype; it can get pricey (dinner entrées from $24), but the *prix fixe* menus are very reasonable (two-course lunch from $13). Specialties include jumbo crabcakes, turtle soup, truffle and wild mushroom stew, and a killer, bread pudding soufflé; at the hugely popular Sunday jazz brunch (from $28), you can enjoy the likes of foie gras pie or eggs Jeannette (poached, with garlic- and black-pepper-crusted pork loins in a rich mushroom and leek sauce with a sage biscuit). Jacket required for dinner and Sunday lunch; no shorts, T-shirts, running shoes, or jeans at any time. Reservations essential.

Juan's Flying Burrito

2018 Magazine St at St Andrew
☎504/569-0000. Mainstay of the Lower Garden District boho scene, with groovy music, local art on the walls, and low, low prices. Star dishes include the overstuffed burritos – go for jerk chicken or vegetables – loaded with sour cream and guacamole. They also offer daily specials and happy-hour deals on bottled beers and margaritas. No reservations.

Lulu's in the Garden

Garden District Hotel, 2203 St Charles Ave at Jackson ☎504/586-9956, ⊛www.lulusinthegarden.com. Breakfast only Mon, breakfast and lunch only Tues. The hotel location of this sweet restaurant may lack charm, but the sunny, unfussy dining room is pleasant, and the simple, fresh food – typical choices include pan-roasted shrimp with lobster mashed potatoes and garlic roast mushrooms – is causing a citywide stir. Dinner entrées start at around $17; lunch is far less expensive.

Uglesich's

1238 Baronne St at Erato ☎504/523-8571. Lunch only. Closed Sat & Sun; closed summer. Shabby seafood joint, two blocks from the streetcar just outside the Lower Garden District. Yugoslavian Gail and Anthony Uglesich ("Yewgle-sitch") draw on Eastern European cuisine to create arguably the best food in the city – prices are higher than you might expect from the venue, but they're worth it. Everything is spectacular, from the softshell crabs and crawfish macque choux to the barbecue oyster stew and the phenomenal sizzling shrimp Gail cooked with cayenne. Feast on freshly shucked oysters at the bar while you wait for a seat (which can be a while). No credit cards.

Bars

The Bulldog

3236 Magazine St at Pleasant ☎504/891-1516. Laid-back bar with a thirtysomething crowd and lively local scene at night. The main appeal is the wide range of beers – some fifty on tap and more than 200 in bottles – from around the world. In warm weather the benches out on the street are filled until the wee hours.

Parasol's

2533 Constance St at Third ☎504/897-5413. Anyone in town on or around St Patrick's Day should make a beeline for this Irish bar – their street parade is a blast, awash with green beer, green beads, and green-haired revelers. The rest of the year, it's a welcoming neighborhood spot, with good roast-beef po-boys, boudin sandwiches, and sport on the TV.

Live music and clubs

Twiropa

1544 Tchoupitoulas at Orange ☎504/522-1544, ⊛www.twiropa.com. Huge music venue in an old industrial building with six stages and eight bars, featuring live music from Latin to grunge rock, and a variety of DJ nights, including high-energy, alternative, and fetish parties.

Performing arts

Zeitgeist Multi-Disciplinary Arts Center

1724 Oretha Castle Haley Blvd at Felicity ☎504/525-2767, ⊛www.zeitgeistinc.org. Volunteer-run, non-profit arts center sharing space with the offbeat Barrister's folk art gallery. One of the city's few truly alternative venues, it's a great place for movies (lots of gay, lesbian, avant-garde, and world cinema), underground music, political poetry, performance art, theater, lectures, workshops, and readings. Cover from $6.

Uptown

Although most tourists see little more of it than the Garden District (see p.134), uptown New Orleans covers a vast chunk of the city, extending roughly between Jackson and Carrollton avenues. While Uptown is a mixed area, the stately, live-oak-lined St Charles Avenue is its showpiece boulevard, studded with fabulous mansions. These are best seen from the historic St Charles streetcar, which then brings you to peaceful Audubon Park and its zoo (also reachable by riverboat from the French Quarter). Beyond the park, the track turns sharply inland to the studenty Riverbend area, where a cluster of great bars and restaurants lie on and around Carrollton Avenue. Uptown's other main artery is Magazine Street, whose unique stores, galleries, restaurants, and bars extend as far as Clay Avenue, a couple of blocks short of the park. While it's perfectly safe to walk Magazine's uptown stretch, you may get a little footsore.

St Charles Avenue

Beyond the Garden District, swanky St Charles Avenue offers a great view of a variety of architectural styles, from Italianate to Romanesque to Queen Anne. Many of the mansions here – including his own little Queen Anne gingerbread home at no. 4010 (riverside) – are the work of the eminent Thomas Sully, also responsible for some of the most important buildings in the CBD.

You can hardly miss the Brown House, a limestone Romanesque monster at no. 4717 (lakeside); it's the largest mansion on the avenue. Further along, at no. 5705 (lakeside), look out for the gleaming white 1941 replica of

Tara, Scarlett's beloved home in *Gone With the Wind*; close on its heels at no. 5809 (lakeside), the aptly nicknamed Wedding Cake House is an ostentatious Greek Revival building, frosted with a layer of balconies, balustrades, cornices, and columns. Beyond, the handsome university campuses of Loyola and Tulane (lakeside) stand side by side facing Audubon Park.

Audubon Park

Built on plantation lands once belonging to Etienne de Boré – who in 1795 perfected the sugar granulation process, and went on to become the city's first mayor – Upper City Park was laid

Lakeside and riverside

Owing to the strange geography of their city, New Orleanians don't use compass directions. Instead, when something is referred to as riverside, it means it lies towards the Mississippi; lakeside is, of course, the side nearer the lake. See p.187 for more details.

▲ HANGING OUT IN AUDUBON PARK

out in 1871. After hosting the 1884 Cotton Exposition, which marked the onset of a nascent tourist industry in New Orleans, the park was redeveloped and renamed for celebrated naturalist John James Audubon, who stayed in the city in 1821 while compiling his seminal *Birds of America*. Today the 350-acre Audubon Park is a lovely, much-used space, dotted with lagoons and picnic areas, shaded by Spanish-moss-swathed trees and looped by an extensive cycling and jogging path.

Audubon Zoo

Summer Mon–Fri 9.30am–5pm, Sat & Sun 9.30am–6pm; rest of year daily 9.30am–5pm. $11, children $6; zoo and aquarium $20/11; zoo, aquarium and boat cruise $34/16.50; see p.98 for other combination tickets. The best thing about Audubon Zoo – a fifteen-minute walk or short shuttle ride (9.30am–5pm; every 20–30min) from the park's St Charles entrance – is its beautifully re-created Louisiana swamp, complete with Cajun houseboats, wallowing alligators, and knobbly cypress knees poking out of the emerald green water. Animals here include raccoons, otters, bears, cougars, and the broadhead skink, Louisiana's largest lizard. If the snakes and reptiles leave you cold, you can take refuge with the fluffy bobcat kittens in the cozy swamp nursery.

Star of the swamp, is, of course, the alligator, and you'll find many things gator-related here, from monstrous prehistoric skulls to the tank of tiny hatchlings perched precariously on small logs. The main attraction is the mysterious blue-eyed white alligator named Mr Bingle – one of eighteen

▼ MR BINGLE AT THE ZOO

Uptown PLACES

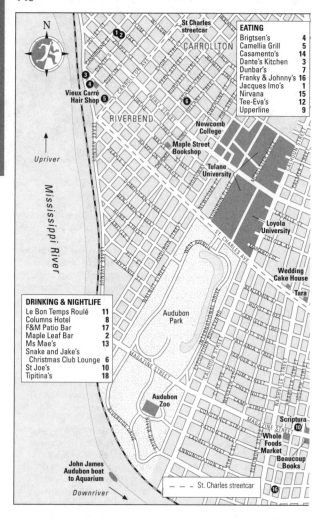

N

St Charles
streetcar

CARROLLTON

EATING

Brigtsen's	4
Camellia Grill	5
Casamento's	14
Dante's Kitchen	3
Dunbar's	7
Franky & Johnny's	16
Jacques Imo's	1
Nirvana	15
Tee-Eva's	12
Upperline	9

Vieux Carré
Hair Shop

RIVERBEND

Newcomb
College

Maple Street
Bookshop

Tulane
University

Upriver

Mississippi River

Loyola
University

Wedding
Cake House

Tara

DRINKING & NIGHTLIFE

Le Bon Temps Roulé	11
Columns Hotel	8
F&M Patio Bar	17
Maple Leaf Bar	2
Ms Mae's	13
Snake and Jake's Christmas Club Lounge	6
St Joe's	10
Tipitina's	18

Audubon
Park

Scriptura

Whole
Foods
Market

Beaucoup
Books

Audubon
Zoo

John James
Audubon boat
to Aquarium

— — — St. Charles streetcar

Downriver

leucistic hatchlings discovered by a Cajun fisherman in a nearby swamp in 1987. No one knows what causes their milky coloring, and as yet these are the only such creatures ever found. At the barn-like swamp café, you can eat gumbo and crawfish pie seated in a rocking chair on the veranda; look carefully and you'll see the enormous snapping turtles just beneath the water's surface.

Some of the zoo's other re-created habitats, despite their lush vegetation and pleasant boardwalks, are showing their age. Best bets are the African savannah, where along with the hippos, leopards, and giraffes,

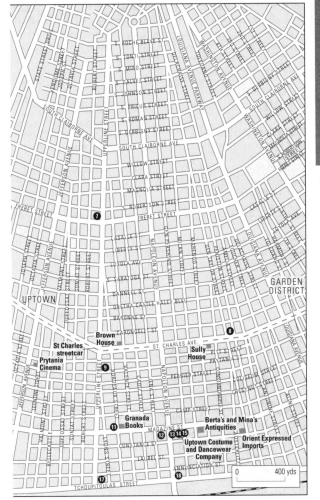

Monkey Hill (which at 27.5ft is proudly labeled as the highest natural point in the city), provides an informal staggered splash pool for overheated kids in summer, and Jaguar Jungle, where jaguars, sloths, anteaters, and monkeys prowl, doze, snuffle, and swing among mock Mayan ruins. Look out too for the komodo dragons, and, in the Asian Domain the rare white tiger, who like the alligator is white, with blue eyes. Anyone with kids should make a beeline for the cheery carousel of endangered species ($2), near the river entrance; the toy train that weaves through the zoo also leaves from here ($3).

The John James Audubon riverboat

A highly appealing way to get to or from the zoo – perhaps combining it with a streetcar ride in the opposite direction – is to take a narrated cruise on the *John James Audubon* riverboat, which plies the Mississippi between the zoo and the aquarium. For details, see p.99.

Shops

Beaucoup Books

5414 Magazine St at Jefferson ⊕504/895-2663. New fiction – including many titles by local authors – as well as cookbooks, art books, Granta periodicals, and foreign-language titles. It hosts frequent author readings.

Berta's and Mina's Antiquities

4138 Magazine St at Milan ⊕504/895-6201. Misleadingly named store crammed with the inventive folk art of Nicaraguan-born Nilo Lanzas, who started painting

at the age of 63. His brash dioramas, many of them painted on old wooden windowframes, portray quirky biblical and rural scenes, or depict life in the imaginary town of Niloville, all of them daubed with witty, touching captions.

Granada Books

4729 Magazine St at Bordeaux ⊕504/891-2626. Closed Mon. This shabby warren of a place is a treasure-trove of used books in every category; it's also something of a neighborhood hangout for local bohemians. Help yourself to coffee in the tiny back room and take it out into the funky back garden. Also offers Internet access ($6/hr; 15min minimum).

Maple Street Book Shop

7523 Maple St at Cherokee ⊕504/866-4916. Beloved Riverbend store housed in a homey, tumbledown cottage in a jasmine-filled garden. Lots of local titles – classic and contemporary – history books and a great art/photography selection, with frequent book signings and searches for hard-to-find titles. The same people own the children's bookshop next door.

Orient Expressed Imports

3905 Magazine St at General Taylor ⊕504/899-3060. Closed Sun. Eclectic, sprawling shop that sells unusual antiques and imports, including Mexican wooden *santo* figures, masks and icons, Thai buddhas, and ancient Chinese figurines.

▼ MAPLE STREET BOOK SHOP

Scriptura

5423 Magazine St at Octavia
☏504/897-1555. Closed Sun. Delicate
handmade notebooks, art
papers, rich inks, classy writing
paper, and designer cards, plus a
selection of butter-soft leather
journals and address books.

Uptown Costume and Dancewear Company

4326 Magazine St at Napoleon
☏504/895-7969. Closed Sun.
Big fancy-dress store packed
tight with inexpensive wigs,
masks, costumes, hats, shoes,
accessories, and make-up. Staff
are informative and helpful,
even when rushed off their
feet during Mardi Gras (when
the place is milling with krewe
members and marching bands)
and Halloween (stage make-up
and hideous latex heads are
particularly popular). Opening
hours are extended during these
busy periods.

Vieux Carré Hair Shop

8224 Maple St at Dante ☏504/862-
6936. Closed Sun. Whether you're
after a plastic pig face or Mickey
Mouse hands, you'll find them
in this friendly, family-owned
theatrical supplier, somewhat
incongruously set in a pretty
Riverbend cottage. Shelves
of decrepit polystyrene heads
sporting off-center woollen wigs,
beards, sideburns, and lashes
share space with false bosoms
and bottoms, stage make-up and
feather boas, with a nice line in
rubber masks and false noses.

Whole Foods Market

5600 Magazine St at Joseph
☏504/899-9119. Vast, bustling
supermarket with a fabulous
range of take-out food, including
boiled seafood, sushi, artisan
breads, fresh sandwiches (try
the blackened catfish po-boy),

wheat-free chocolate fudge cake,
and, to top it all a coffee stand
serving good café au lait.

Restaurants

Brigtsen's

723 Dante St at Leake ☏504/861-
7610, ⊕www.brigtsens.com. Closed
Sun & Mon. Gourmet restaurant
serving dinner only spread across
a handful of cozy rooms in an
old Riverbend house. The long,
handwritten menu of hearty
Creole-Cajun dishes changes
daily; of the entrées ($15–30)
the seafood is especially good,
whether served in a gumbo or
fragrant bisque (try the shrimp
and butternut variety), blackened,
or smothered in creamy sauces.
You can't go wrong with
rabbit tenderloin, either, served
with Creole mustard sauce.
Reservations advised.

Camellia Grill

626 S Carrollton Ave at Hampson
☏504/866-9573. Breakfast & lunch
only. Housed in a crumbling,
columned Riverbend building,
this classic chrome-and-formica
diner has become an institution
for fast-fried food – lines can be
long, especially at weekends. A
maître d' seats you on leatherette
banquettes until a stool becomes
free at the double-horseshoe
counter; there, brisk waitstaff
bark your orders to the cooks
frying right behind them. You're
here more for the ambience
than the food – though the
chilli cheese omelette, with
potato and onion, packs a
punch. No credit cards.

Casamento's

4330 Magazine St at Napoleon
☏504/895-9761. Mid-Sept to May;
closed Mon. Spotless, wonderfully
old-fashioned oyster bar – all

cream, aqua, and floral tiles – that's been going since 1919. Other than the oysters, shucked at the marble bar (try them with a grilled cheese sandwich on the side), good choices include the fried crab claws or the trout "loaf," a buttery, overstuffed sandwich made with hunks of white bread. Friendly and bustling, this is an unmissable New Orleans experience. No credit cards.

Dante's Kitchen

736 Dante St at Leake ☎504/861-3121. Classy New Creole cuisine served in a cozy Riverbend shotgun. Star appetizers include crabmeat and Brie French toast or duck confit and root vegetable hashcake, while of the entrées ($14–24) the falafel-crusted Gulf fish and the portobello mushroom with green curry are good bets. Prices are lower at lunch, when you can eat a variety of salads and sandwiches on the sunny patio, or at the weekend brunches. Reservations advised for dinner.

Dunbar's

4927 Freret St at Upperline ☎504/899-0734. Closed Sun. Family-run, friendly, and inexpensive little neighborhood place dishing up spectacular Creole soul food. Gut-busting breakfasts – pork chops, French toast, smoked sausage, grits, and biscuits – will keep you going all day; at lunch or dinner, go for red beans and rice (the house specialty), meatloaf (Wed only) or fried chicken with mustard greens, candied yams, and cornbread.

Franky & Johnny's

321 Arabella St at Tchoupitoulas ☎504/899-9146. This homely, noisy neighborhood Italian-American restaurant – with

red checked tablecloths, sassy waitresses, and Italian crooners and New Orleans R&B on the jukebox – gets packed at weekends with families and large parties. Food is downhome Cajun-Creole – turtle soup, alligator pie, gumbo, softshell crabs, boiled crawfish, stuffed artichoke, and the like – and their po-boys are consistently voted best in the city.

Jacques Imo's

8324 Oak St at Dante ☎504/861-0886. Closed Sun. The quirky, rowdy bar and wildly colorful covered patio at this superb Riverbend restaurant are a little at odds with the cuisine, an inventive, gourmet Creole-Caribbean take on soul food. Everything on the long menu – garlicky fried oysters, chicken livers, buttery blackened redfish with champagne Brie sauce, ambrosial alligator cheesecake, smothered rabbit with cornbread dressing, to name but a few – is outstanding. Sides include macque choux, sweet potatoes, or butterbeans with rice – you'll leave feeling stuffed. It's the place to eat before a gig at the *Maple Leaf* (see p.152), but they don't accept reservations for parties smaller than five, so settle down at the bar for a long wait.

Nirvana

4308 Magazine St at General Pershing ☎504/894-9797. Closed Mon. This lovely looking Indian restaurant serves authentic food ranging from Goan dishes to biryani and tandoori to creative fusions. Vegetarian choices are good: go for the potato patties topped with curried garbanzo beans, the naurattan curry with vegetables and creamy paneer, or a thali. Entrées start at $11; the lunch buffet is great value at $6.95.

Tee-Eva's

4430 Magazine St at Napoleon
℡504/899-8350. Tee-Eva, who used to sing backing vocals for the late Ernie K-Doe (see p.119), runs this colorful take-out stand, dishing out sno-balls, the sugary crushed-ice treat that New Orleanians go mad for, along with scrumptious pecan pralines and sweet potato pies. You can call ahead to order a $6 plate lunch (fried catfish, red beans and rice, and so on).

Upperline

1413 Upperline St at Prytania
℡504/891-9822, ⊛www.upperline .com. Closed Mon. Romantic, cheerful restaurant filled with a jumble of bright paintings, prints, and ceramics. Of the contemporary Creole food try the fried green tomatoes with shrimp rémoulade or crispy sweetbreads to start, followed by roast duck with garlic port, or grilled Gulf fish with warm salade niçoise and tapenade. The reasonably priced Taste of New Orleans sampler gets you seven specialties, including warm bread pudding, for $35. Reservations recommended.

Bars

Columns Hotel Bar

3811 St Charles Ave at General Taylor
℡504/899-9308. This gorgeous hotel (see p.182), on the edge of the Garden District, has an old bar, richly decorated in dark wood and faded velvet. You can drink in a number of rooms, all of which exude faded grandeur with their chandeliers, Baroque mirrors, and vases of plump pink roses; on warm evenings, customers make for the columned veranda, which overlooks the St Charles streetcar line. Free snacks on Friday evenings, and live Latin, jazz, and piano Mon–Wed.

F&M Patio Bar

4841 Tchoupitoulas St at Lyons
℡504/895-6784. A favorite on the post-*Tipitina's* circuit since the 1960s, this friendly, drunken,

▼ TEE-EVA'S

local hangout has it all – pool tables, a patio, great jukebox, and cholesterol-packed snacks served until late. Traditionally it's *de rigueur* to guzzle Bloody Marys and dance on the pool table, but no one will mind if you don't.

Ms Mae's

4336 Magazine St at Napoleon ☎504/895-9401. Another post-*Tipitina's* haunt, open 24hr, which attracts a mixed crowd of serious-drinking locals and students. The atmosphere is less frenetic than at F&M, and the pool table sees more cue balls than pratfalls, but it's still very lively, especially at weekends.

Snake and Jake's Christmas Club Lounge

7612 Oak St at Hillary ☎504/861-2802. Distinctive drinking hole in a tumbledown shack with perennial Yuletide decorations fading in the gloom. Nothing much happens before 2am, when it fills up with a jubilant local crowd of musicians, journalists, and students. The

jukebox is superb, with a playlist of New Orleans music, classic soul, and R&B.

St Joe's

5535 Magazine St at Joseph ☎504/899-3744. The decor at this neighborhood bar is exotic – Oriental lanterns, Indonesian dolls, folk art crosses, shrunken heads – but the atmosphere is down-to-earth, with a friendly, mixed crowd of locals enjoying the nice candlelit patio, the pool table, and the jumping jukebox (lots of swing and Latin).

Live music and clubs

Le Bon Temps Roulé

4801 Magazine St at Bordeaux ☎504/895-8117. A spirited mix of locals and hard-drinking students fill this attractive, convivial neighborhood bar – the name is a variation on the Cajun phrase "laissez les bon temps rouler", or "let the good times roll." The wildly popular trumpet stylist Kermit Ruffins plays every Wednesday, with the hip brass bands ReBirth on Friday and Soul Rebels on Saturday – other nights it's a mixed bag of blues, acoustic, funk, jazz, zydeco, R&B, or rock. They also offer food specials – free oysters, red beans and rice, and such like – a wide selection of beers, two pool tables, a great jukebox, and a patio. Usually no cover.

Maple Leaf Bar

8316 Oak St at Dante ☎504/866-9359. Friendly old bar with pressed-tin walls, a large dancefloor, and a patio. Established for some thirty years, it's an institution much beloved of locals, who

▼ ST JOE'S

fill the place – and the sidewalk outside – for a nightly menu of New Orleans piano, R&B, brass (ReBirth's rambunctious Tuesday-night gigs are legendary), and blues. Cover varies; $8 for ReBirth Brass Band.

Tipitina's

501 Napoleon Ave at Tchoupitoulas ☏504/895-8477, ⊛www.tipitinas .com. Legendary venue, named for a Professor Longhair song and sporting a banner with his likeness above the stage. Though it's no longer the must-see it once was, *Tip's* still has a good line-up of funk, R&B, brass, and reggae, spanning the range from local favorites to national acts. And the Cajun *fais-do-do*, or dance (with free lessons; Sun 5–9pm) is fantastic. Cover varies.

▲ THE MAPLE LEAF BAR

Mid-City

Predominantly residential Mid-City, the large stretch of land that fans up from Tremé toward Lake Pontchartrain, is of interest largely for City Park, its eclectic New Orleans Museum of Art, and the celebrated annual Jazz Fest (see p.193) at the Fair Grounds racetrack. While you may well venture into Mid-City for its restaurants – there's an especially good cluster along Esplanade Avenue – it's not a good idea to wander around the poverty-scarred outskirts of Tremé; bus #48, running from the corner of Rampart in the French Quarter, along Esplanade all the way to City Park, is a safe way to travel during the day, but call a taxi after dark. Alternatively, take the streetcar from Canal Street to the Esplanade Avenue entrance of the park, convenient for the museum and the Pitot House.

Esplanade Avenue

In the antebellum era, wealthy Creoles turned their sights toward Esplanade Avenue, the broad, live-oak-lined street that sweeps up from the Mississippi to City Park. Escaping the congested French Quarter, they lined the grand boulevard with large, fashionable homes, fronting them with voluminous, filigree cast-iron galleries. Today, many of the houses, though hauntingly lovely, are decidedly run-down, and stretches of the road lie blighted and desolate. Restoration, monitored by a vocal preservation group, is gradually improving matters, and a handful of the homes have been converted into luxurious B&Bs, with a nice stretch of restaurants along Esplanade Ridge, the "high" ground (about 4ft above sea level) that hugs either side of the avenue.

Bayou St John

Were it not for Bayou St John, New Orleans might never have existed. Local Indians had long used what was to become today's city as a portage: the alligator-filled bayou, an inlet of Lake Pontchartrain, provided a handy short-cut between the Mississippi and the Gulf of Mexico via the lake, bypassing the river's perilous lower reaches. As the city grew, the countryside around the bayou was carved into plantations worked by African slaves, and in the early 1800s it evolved into a popular gathering place for local voodooists. Though it remained a key waterway until the 1920s, today Bayou St John flows along the edge of City Park and through the heart of a well-heeled residential neighborhood – it's a favorite spot for fishing and dog-walking – with not an alligator to be seen.

St Louis No. 3 Cemetery

3421 Esplanade Ave at Moss. Daily 10am–3pm. Free. Built in 1856 on the site of a leper colony, St Louis No. 3 is a peaceful burial ground used mostly by religious orders; all the priests of the diocese are buried here,

▲ ST LOUIS NO. 3

and fragile angels balance on top of the tombs. It also holds the family tomb of James Gallier Jr, designed by the architect himself, and that of photographer E.J. Bellocq, whose remarkable early twentieth-century images of Storyville's prostitutes have become icons of a lost era. More recently, following a huge jazz funeral in 1999, Mardi Gras Indian Donald Harrison Sr, Chief of the Guardians of the Flame tribe and father of famed jazz saxophonist Donald Harrison Jr, was entombed here (see p.166 for more on the Mardi Gras Indians).

Though St Louis No. 3 is one of the safer of New Orleans' cemeteries, to get the most out of a visit it's still best to take a guided tour; see p.191 for details.

The Pitot House

1440 Moss St at Esplanade. Wed–Sat 10am–3pm. $5. One of the prettiest house museums in New Orleans, the Pitot House stands near the upper end of Esplanade on the banks of the bayou. It's the only remaining West Indies-style plantation home in the city, built in 1799 and named for its second owner, James Pitot, a French merchant who came to the United States fleeing the 1792 slave rebellions in Haiti. Pitot developed one of the city's first cotton presses, and succeeded Etienne de Boré as mayor in 1804. With its stucco-covered walls, ground-floor basement, airy galleries, and double-pitched roof, it's a typical Caribbean-New Orleans structure, and has been decorated in a simple, elegant style true to its period. From the front galleries you get lovely views out over the parterre garden to the bayou, while crops of cotton, indigo, ginger, and bananas form a patchwork across the small back garden. Tours, a lively mix of

▼ PITOT HOUSE

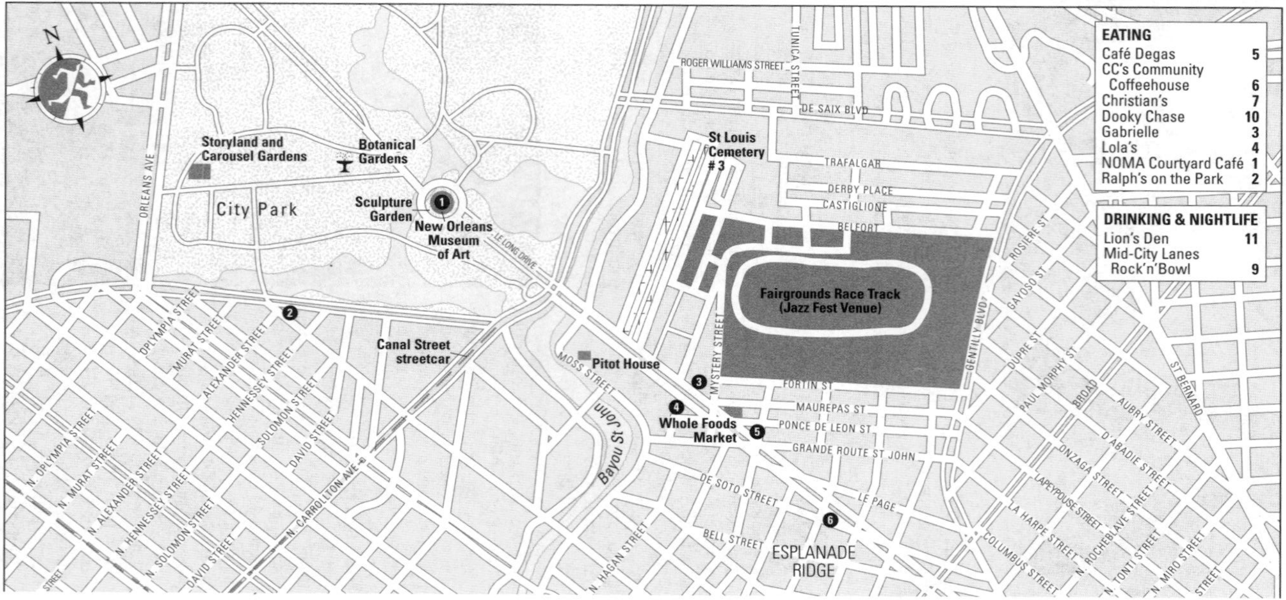

Fairgrounds Race Track
(Jazz Fest Venue)

St Louis Cemetery #3

Whole Foods Market

Pitot House

New Orleans Museum of Art

Sculpture Garden

Botanical Gardens

Storyland and Carousel Gardens

City Park

Canal Street streetcar

Bayou St John

ESPLANADE RIDGE

STREET NAMES: ST BERNARD, AUBRY STREET, D'ABADIE STREET, N TONTI STREET, N MIRO STREET, N ROCHEBLAVE STREET, N DORGENOIS STREET, BROAD, PAUL MURPHY ST, ONZAGA STREET, DUPRE, GAYOSO ST, ROSIERE ST, LA HARPE STREET, N COLUMBUS STREET, LAPEYROUSE STREET, N MIRO STREET, GENTILLY BLVD, TRAFALGAR, DERBY PLACE, CASTIGLIONE, BELFORT, FORTIN ST, MAUREPAS ST, PONCE DE LEON ST, GRANDE ROUTE ST JOHN, LE PAGE, DE SAIX BLVD, DE SOTO STREET, BELL STREET, N HAGAN STREET, MYSTERY STREET, TUNICA STREET, ROGER WILLIAMS STREET, MOSS STREET, ZELLONG DRIVE, ORLEANS AVE, N CARROLLTON AVE, DAVID STREET, N SOLOMON STREET, HENNESSEY STREET, N ALEXANDER STREET, N MURAT STREET, N OLYMPIA STREET, DAVID STREET, N SOLOMON STREET, N ALEXANDER STREET, N HENNESSEY STREET, N MURAT STREET, N OPELMPIA STREET, N SOLOMON STREET

anecdote, historical snippets, and architectural detail, draw your attention to everything from the *briquette entre poteaux* (bricks between posts) construction of the building to the customized food cupboards, their legs planted in bowls of water to confound the ants. Look out, too, for the lush, apricot-colored sofa in the drawing room: the site of an orgy of blood-lust in the movie *Interview with the Vampire*, here it looks rather genteel.

City Park

City Park covers some 1500 acres between Bayou St John and Lake Pontchartrain. Crisscrossed with roads, it's nonetheless an appealing, impressively landscaped green space, streaked with lagoons and shaded by centuries-old live oaks draped in ragged gray beards of Spanish moss. Built in the 1860s, the park expanded in the 1920s, when the Beaux Arts Delgado Museum, now the New Orleans Museum of Art, established itself as the city's most important gallery.

Today the art museum and its sculpture garden remain the chief attraction, though visitors

who've overdone it pounding the streets of the French Quarter can take solace in the atmospheric Art Deco botanical garden, filled with thousands of native plants, including blooming azaleas, magnolias, and camellias. And anyone with young children in tow can head for the Storyland playground (Wed–Fri 10am–12.30pm, Sat & Sun 10am–4.30pm; $2), which, designed in the 1950s, is appealingly dated. Kids also like the neighboring carousel gardens, a small theme park featuring an antique merry-go-round (Wed–Fri 10am–2.30pm, Sat & Sun 11am–4.30pm; $1, plus $1 per ride, $10 unlimited rides). Opening hours of all the park's attractions can vary; call ☎504/482-4888 before you set out.

New Orleans Museum of Art

Tues, Wed & Fri–Sun 10am–5pm, Thurs 12.30–8.30pm. ⊚www.noma.org. $8.
Near the Esplanade entrance to City Park, the New Orleans Museum of Art (NOMA) holds an impressive, wide-ranging collection. Particularly strong are the Asian galleries, where everything from tiny eighth-century Jain bronzes to Zen ink paintings and elaborate suits of Edo armor is precisely exhibited; similarly, the African galleries – a dizzying array of masks, beaded ceremonial costumes, and fetishes – and the Oceanic galleries – which include wizened heads from Papua New Guinea and fierce eighteenth-century Hawaiian temple figures – plot admirably clear courses through their jaw-dropping treasures.

▼ STORYLAND, CITY PARK

NOMA also has an outstanding collection of Fabergé eggs, exquisite pieces of end-of-Empire decadence. Commissioned to make a precious egg for the tsar's daughter, Russian jeweler Peter Carl Fabergé offered an extravagant take on traditional Russian dolls: a silver egg containing a hinged jeweled chicken, sporting a gold crown, which, in turn, hides an emerald ring. It is among those on show here, along with humble dandelions and lilies magically transformed with platinum pods, gold stems, translucent nephrite leaves, and seeds made from infinitesimal diamonds.

Of NOMA's paintings, French artists – naturally – are well represented. Watch out for the imposing portrait of Marie Antoinette by the young court painter Élisabeth-Louise Vigée-Lebrun, and Edgar Degas' 1872 painting of his New Orleans cousin, Estelle Musson – a poignant image of an unseeing woman reaching out to a blazing red gladiola.

NOMA Sculpture Garden

Tues, Wed & Fri–Sun 10am–5pm, Thurs 12.30–8.30pm. Free. To the left of the museum lies the impressive NOMA Sculpture Garden. Set in five landscaped acres of winding paths and lagoons, shaded by fat magnolias, richly scented jasmine, and ragged Spanish moss, many of the sculptures appear to have grown from the ground – one tree, strewn with giant necklaces, wittily evokes New Orleans' bead-bedecked branches left in the wake of Mardi Gras parades (see p.169), while Louise Bourgeois' spindly giant spider seems as organic and gnarled as the venerable live oaks that surround it. Among works by such luminaries as

Barbara Hepworth, Magritte, and Henry Moore, Alison Saar's chilling *Travelin' Light* leaves a lasting impression – an African-American figure, cast in brass and hanging by his feet from a gallows, it tolls like a bell when you pull a chain at the back, its mournful call resounding through the park.

Shops

Whole Foods Market

3135 Esplanade Ave at Ponce de Leon ☎504/943-1626. Health-food supermarket with a good, though not inexpensive, deli counter serving smoothies, salads, and sandwiches that you can bundle up for a picnic in the park. Hot food includes chunky vegetable soups, lasagne, and baked eggplant.

Cafés

CC's Community Coffeehouse

2800 Esplanade Ave at De Soto ☎504/482-9865. Excellent neighborhood coffeehouse, with lots of peaceful outdoor seating under Esplanade's enormous live oaks, free WiFi access, and good coffee and snacks to boot.

NOMA Courtyard Café

City Park. Closed Mon. A peaceful refuelling spot, serving coffee, drinks, and tasty light meals, with big picture windows overlooking City Park's trees and lagoons.

Restaurants

Café Degas

3127 Esplanade Ave at Ponce de Leon. ☎504/945-5635. Closed lunch Mon. Cozy little French-style bistro, with a covered deck, serving well-executed classics such as warm goat cheese salad, onion soup, snails, and roasted duck to a contented, laid-back local crowd. If you're on a budget, come for the three-course *prix fixe* (Mon–Thurs 5.30–7pm $16.99, 7–10pm $19.99).

Christian's

3835 Iberville St at N Cortez ☎504/482-4924, ⊛www .christiansrestaurantneworleans.com. Closed Sun & lunch Sat. Just a block from the Canal Street streetcar, in an elegantly restored Lutheran church – the stained glass and vaulted ceilings are still intact – this local favorite serves very good French-Creole food including smoked softshell crab, flash-fried oysters en brochette, saffron bouillabaisse, and seafood-stuffed filet steak. It's not cheap – dinner will set you back at least $40 a head – but during their early-evening specials (Tues–Thurs 5.30–6.30pm) you can get three courses for less than $25.

Dooky Chase's

2301 Orleans Ave at Miro ☎504/821-0600. Classy black Creole food dished up in a refined dining room (incongruously set in a blighted neighborhood) favored by movers and shakers in the city's black community. Of the entrées ($10–18), the crispy fried chicken, oyster-stuffed chicken breast, and gumbo – made with chicken, ham veal, crab, shrimp, and spicy and smoked sausage – are all amazing. And for a side, the sweet potatoes are meltingly good. For the best value, go for the freshly made lunch buffet (Mon–Fri $12.95), or, for dinner, the Creole feast ($37.50). The area is dangerous; take a cab.

Gabrielle

3201 Esplanade Ave at Mystery ☎504/948-6233. Dinner only Tues–Thurs & Sat, closed Sun & Mon. This tiny triangle of a restaurant has a justified reputation for its delicious contemporary Cajun-Creole cuisine. Traditional-sounding dishes come with a creative spin: go for a plate of grilled sausages, barbecue shrimp pie, cracker-crusted rabbit, or panéed veal with sautéed oysters, and make sure to leave room for the stunning home-made desserts. Lunch on Friday, three courses for $18.95, is a bargain.

▼ DOOKY CHASE'S

▲ PAELLA AT LOLA'S

the park and its wrought-iron gate. The food, like the dining room itself, is minimal and tasteful – try the mussel soup, simple baked drum served with steamed rice, and theobrama, a rich chocolate soup – and the views are great, of course. It can get noisy at lunchtime; dinners are more relaxing.

Live music and clubs

Lion's Den

544 S Broad Ave at Gravier ☎504/821-3745. Tiny club part-owned by R&B legend Irma Thomas, who performs very occasionally, usually during festivals (check listings papers, or call), when they also put on beans and rice for her devoted fans. Take a taxi. Cover varies.

Mid-City Lanes Rock'n'Bowl

4133 S Carrollton Ave at Tulane ☎504/482-3133, ⊛www.rockandbowl .com. Joyful, rambunctious, and carefree, this eccentric ten-lane bowling alley-cum-live music venue is pure New Orleans, and fantastic fun. Wednesday and Thursday nights are zydeco nights, when such greats as Geno Delafose and Rosie Ledet stir the local, jubilant, hard-dancing crowd into such a frenzy that you can barely hear the crashing of the pins. Other nights they book good local R&B, blues, Latin, and swamp pop. Tues–Sat only, except during festivals; cover varies.

Lola's

3312 Esplanade Ave at Mystery ☎504/488-6946. Noisy, colorful little place serving dinner that has become a firm local favorite for mouthwatering, cheap, and authentic Spanish food. To start, choose from lentil or garlic soup, gazpacho, or lip-licking grilled shrimp, perhaps following with grilled rack of lamb. Star turns, however, are the paellas, cooked to order in the open kitchen, served in a cast-iron skillet and packed with seafood, meat, or vegetables, or all three. Fresh bread comes warm, with garlic-packed butter. No reservations, so arrive early or wait, and no credit cards. BYOB.

Ralph's on the Park

900 City Park Ave at Dumaine ☎504/485-1000, ⊛www .ralphsonthepark.com. Closed dinner Sun. Classy Ralph Brennan-owned restaurant right opposite

Mardi Gras

Already one of the liveliest cities in North America, New Orleans lurches into an irresistible frenzy during carnival season, which starts on Twelfth Night and runs for the six weeks or so until Ash Wednesday. Though the name defines the entire season, Mardi Gras itself – an official holiday – French for "Fat Tuesday," is simply the culmination of a whirl of parades, parties, bohemian street revels, and secret masked balls, all inextricably tied up with the city's byzantine social, racial, and political structures. It's hard to imagine another city in the developed world that could, for more than a month, devote all its energy and resources to the simple pursuit of pleasure – yet while it's by far the busiest tourist season, when the city is invaded by millions of people, Mardi Gras has always been, above all, a party that New Orleanians throw for themselves. Visitors are wooed, welcomed, and shown the time of their lives, but without them carnival would reel on regardless, dressing wildly, drinking, and dancing its bizarre way into Lent.

Some history

Mardi Gras was brought to New Orleans in the 1740s by French colonists who continued the European custom, established since medieval times, of marking the imminence of Lent with partying, masking, and feasting. Their slaves, meanwhile, celebrated African and Caribbean festival traditions, based on musical rituals and the donning of elaborate costumes. All over the city, street parades would descend into rowdy affairs, with masked revelers flinging flour, mud, and bricks.

Official Mardi Gras took its current form in 1857, when a mysterious torchlit procession, calling itself the "Mistick Krewe of Comus, Merrie Monarch

▼ MASKED REVELLERS

of Mirth," took to the streets, initiated by a group of wealthy, white Anglo-Americans. Comus was an all-male, secret society, and its parade was strictly members-only. Based on the theme of Milton's *Paradise Lost*, it featured elaborate floats and masked riders dressed as the demon actors of the epic – very different from the earlier, wilder processions.

Almost immediately, the concept of the krewe, a secret carnival club whose mythological name afforded it a spurious gravitas, was taken up enthusiastically by the Anglo elite. More and more krewes were formed, each electing their own king and queen – usually an older businessman and a debutante – who, costumed and masked, and attended by a fairytale court, would reign over a themed parade and a ceremonial ball, centered on that great nineteenth-century obsession, the tableau vivant.

As the secret krewes grew, street masking and public balls – "unofficial" carnival – became the domain of the poor, the black, and the fallen women. Though official carnival trailed off during the Civil War, it gathered strength during the city's violent Reconstruction era, dominated by the white supremacists whose resistance to the Reconstruction government often exploded into violence. In 1872, newspapers published an arcane announcement heralding the imminent

▲ FRENCH QUARTER

arrival of a "King of Carnival," ordaining that, "under penalty of Royal displeasure," the city be closed down for the day and handed over to him. On Mardi Gras morning, the masked Rex arrived by riverboat to preside over a brilliantly executed parade, which, though it boasted none of the dazzling floats created by Comus, featured hundreds of maskers and mounted horsemen.

Mardi Gras is always the day before Ash Wednesday, exactly 47 days before Easter: in 2005 it falls on Feb 8, in 2006 on Feb 28, and in 2007 it's on Feb 20.

Despite his claim to be "king" of carnival, Rex himself, usually a philanthropist or public leader – and always born in New Orleans – bowed to the venerable Comus. Comus and Rex, along with newly formed krewes Proteus and the satirical, right-wing Knights of Momus, came to dominate organized carnival, their self-appointed monarchs sweeping through crowds of subjects on parades that often used romantic, exotic, and exalted themes to attack Northern politicians and the newly emancipated blacks.

Meanwhile, unofficial carnival reeled on: a number of smaller, informal groups satirized the pomposity of the big krewes and more than once the Comus parade was blocked by jeering hordes. The underworld held its own masques, or "French balls": raucous, drunken affairs that were curtailed in 1917 in part of a city clean-up campaign that included the closure of the notorious Storyville red-light district.

Throughout much of the nineteenth century, the role of black New Orleanians in official carnival was limited to that of torch-carrier, float-hauler, or band-member. Blacks had always celebrated carnival within their own communities, however, and in the 1880s, groups of black men began to organize themselves into Mardi Gras Indian tribes (see p.166), leading their own, often violent, processions through local neighborhoods. Though formal black carnival clubs were known from as early as the 1890s, Zulu, the best-known black krewe, was established in 1909, when a band of laborers formed a benevolent society, called themselves The Tramps, and paraded with a king dressed in rags. At the same time, gangs of poor black women, many of them prostitutes, went out on the town as Baby Dolls, prancing through the streets in satin bloomers and bonnets, and sucking pacifiers. Though most of the Dolls had disappeared by the end of the century, the last couple of Mardi Gras have seen their welcome return, spearheaded by Ernie K-Doe's widow, Antoinette, and featuring some of the earliest Dolls along with scores of eager young hipsters. A similar resurgence has occurred for Tremé's Skeletons; sporting oversized *papier-mâché* skulls, these

▼ SUPER KREWE PARADE

"Bone Gangs" parade through Tremé early on Mardi Gras morning just as they did in the 1920s and 1930s.

In 1916, the Tramps, now the Zulu Social Aid and Pleasure Club, paraded in black-face on palmetto-shaded floats. Lampooning white carnival, and reclaiming black stereotypes, by the 1940s Zulu had become one of the most important black organizations in America. In 1949, local boy Louis Armstrong, who had left the city as a young man, rode as king, an appearance that pushed Mardi Gras, and the city, into the public eye. Today Zulu is one of New Orleans' biggest krewes, and its Mardi Gras Day parade, a raucous cavalcade of black-face savages in wild Afro wigs, is among the most popular of the season.

After a hiatus during World War I, when masking was banned as potentially subversive and the organized krewes stopped parading, carnival was revived during the Jazz Age. By 1925, Rex, Comus, Momus, and Proteus were parading once more, while crowds of citizens took to dancing in the streets, accompanied by small jazz bands on motorized trucks. Many of the official parades also featured brass bands, followed by dancing Second Liners. Proteus, Comus, and Rex continued to parade throughout the Depression; meanwhile, newer krewes, like Hermes, were being formed to attract tourists to carnival.

In 1941 the Krewe of Venus was the first female krewe to parade, dodging the heckles and food hurled at them by the crowds. The early 1960s saw the first gay carnival ball, thrown by the Krewe of Yuga, which was raided by the police. In 1969,

▲ BOURBON STREET

when the city was facing one of its most difficult economic periods, Bacchus emerged on the scene – a very different kind of krewe. Less concerned with exclusivity than with cheerful excess, Bacchus's debut parade boasted the biggest floats, a widely trumpeted celebrity king (Danny Kaye), and, in place of the hush-hush ball, a public extravaganza open to anyone who could afford a ticket. Thus began the era of the colossal super krewes, with members drawn from the ranks of New Orleans' new wealth who were barred from making inroads into the gentlemen's-club network of the old-guard krewes. Super krewe parades are characterized by expensive, flashy floats, alight with state-of-the-art fiber optics. Riders – 2000 of them in the five-hour-long Endymion parade alone – are known for their generous throws (see p.169). Other super krewes include the racially mixed Orpheus, established by Harry Connick Jr in 1993, which always boasts the longest string of marching bands (around thirty of them) and a number of celebrity riders.

In 1992, the city government instigated a nondiscrimination policy for the parading krewes, requiring that, in order to be granted a parade license, they sign affidavits affirming that their organizations were open to all people, regardless of race or religion. While the super krewes agreed to the new conditions – as did Rex – Comus, along with Momus and Proteus, refused to comply, insisting that their membership be kept secret. From 1992 until 1999, none of them paraded, though they continued to stage their elaborate balls, as exclusive and all-white as ever; in 2000, Proteus finally backed down, and has since taken a prime Lundi Gras parade slot.

Unofficial carnival

While official carnival is hardly staid, and certainly not without satire (the krewes of Chaos, Saturn, Muses, and d'Etat in particular are known for the biting wit of their parades), the spirit of old Mardi Gras, when maskers took to the streets to create their own parades and parties, is kept alive today in the city's many unofficial krewes. In addition to the exquisite Krewe of St Ann (see p.171), chief among them is the anarchic Krewe du Vieux (from Vieux Carré, another name for the French Quarter). Their irreverent ball, "the Krewe du Vieux Doo" – basically a wild party, open to all – is the first of the season, starting with a weird and wonderful night-time march that weaves its way from the Faubourg through the French Quarter. Makeshift costumes and bizarre mule-hauled mini-floats satirize current local affairs and scandals, while the city's funkiest brass bands blast the roofs off and hip, artsy marching bands strut and twirl. As usual with New Orleans' walking parades, anyone is welcome to join in, and within minutes the krewe members are trailing in a raggle-taggle Second Line. Tickets for the ball can be bought from the Louisiana Music Factory in the Quarter (see p.64). Uptown, the Krewe of OAK's parade (read: bar crawl) climaxes at the *Maple Leaf* (see p.152) for live music and food well into the early hours. Costumes reveal as much flesh as possible, as the krewe's name ("Outrageous And Kinky") suggests.

And then there's the Mystic Krewe of Barkus, made up of dogs, more than a thousand of whom gather in Louis Armstrong Park in the morning before their proud trot through the French Quarter – all spiffed up on some spurious theme (Saturday Bite Fever, say, or perhaps Fistful of Collars), and presided over by their own king and queen. The dogs, along with owners and onlookers, then stop by the *Good Friends* gay bar (see p.97) to be toasted by city officials before scampering off to a happy party in Louis Armstrong Park.

Mardi Gras Indians

New Orleans' Mardi Gras Indians are not, in fact, Native Americans, but low-income black men who organize themselves into tribes, or "gangs." Today there are some 25 tribes, each with between ten and fifty members, who, on Mardi Gras morning ("that day" in Indian parlance) parade through their local neighborhoods, debuting the extravagant beaded costumes and feathered headdresses that they've spent the last year making. Though there are reports of groups of New Orleans blacks "masking Indian" as early as 1872, the standard story starts in the 1880s, when Becate Battiste, of Native American and African blood, turned up in a bar in Tremé with a bunch of friends and introduced themselves as the "Creole Wild West". Why the practice spread is unclear: some say it developed out of a widespread craze for all things Native American after the 1884 Buffalo Bill Wild West show, while others see it in the broader context of black masking traditions throughout the New World.

The first New Orleans Indians dressed simply and fought gang wars on designated "battlefronts." Since the 1950s, however, they have competed instead with dances and chants and for the "prettiest" costume. These "suits" – which are worn in layers, so sections can be revealed one by one – can weigh as much as 100lb, their tunics, leggings, and moccasins heavy with beads and rhinestones (favored by the Uptown gangs) and sequins (Downtown style). Each ensemble is topped with a towering plumed headdress known as a crown; those worn by the Big Chiefs, quivering with more than 350 feathers, are colossal. Traditionally, suits, painstakingly designed and hand-sewn by the Indians at

▲ MARDI GRAS INDIANS

a cost of thousands of dollars, aren't recycled from one Mardi Gras to the next, though they will be worn again at gigs and special events.

Gangs set out from Big Chief's home early on Mardi Gras morning, led by the spy boy, who looks out for other tribes, and the flag boy, who alerts the chief when his rivals come into view. When tribes meet – usually swamped by now with Second Line crowds – they gather in circles and communicate with dances, hand gestures, percussion-rattling, and improvised calls-and-responses, which go on until Big Chief signals for it all to stop. Influenced by Native American, Haitian, and African chants, and peppered with mysterious pidgin and patois, the songs lament lost tribe members, recall past battles, and brag about fine

▲ DISCARDED MARDI GRAS BEADS

suits. Mardi Gras Indian music has been a key influence on the New Orleans sound, and many famous carnival records, including the much-covered favorites *Iko Iko* and *Hey Pocky Way*, were originally Indian compositions.

Tribes parade through local neighborhoods where tourists, although tolerated, aren't particularly welcome. If you are determined to catch them, try the Backstreet Cultural Museum (see p.116) early in the morning, or wait for the gangs to gather in the late afternoon at Claiborne and Elysian Fields downtown, or LaSalle and Washington uptown. Many of the more famous groups – the Wild Magnolias, in particular, led by the foghorn-voiced Big Chief Bo Dollis – play gigs around town in the run-up to carnival. Don't miss these; the Indians' chest-thumping blend of funk, African beats, and New Orleans party music is some of the best dance music you're likely to hear.

The parades

More than sixty krewes organize major parades in the weeks leading up to the big day: huge, overblown events based around a theme (and using lots of spurious jokes and rotten puns), these can last for hours, featuring marching bands and dancers, colorful, motorized floats, and masked, costumed riders hurling "throws" (see box, opposite) to the shrieking hordes. Though they occur throughout the city, the biggest parades head downtown and attract hundreds of thousands of people. The crowds, and the size of the floats, make it impossible for the parades to pass through the French Quarter; they head instead along broader, safer roads such as Canal and St Charles. Parades increase in number as the season goes on; the busiest days are the two weekends before Mardi Gras itself.

Parades follow routes of up to

Surviving Mardi Gras

You need stamina to survive Mardi Gras, which gets increasingly frenzied as it progresses. For the most fun, you'll want to go with the flow: catch a couple of the big parades, rifle the thrift stores and costume outlets for disguises and masks (you'll feel left out if you don't), keep your eyes open for flyers, and listen to the local radio (WWOZ; see p.189) for news of the best gigs and parties. Official events and parade schedules are advertised in the press and in the widely available glossy handbook *Arthur Hardy's Mardi Gras Guide*. For details of unofficial carnival events, check the listings papers *Offbeat* and *Gambit* (see p.189) and keep your eyes open in the hippest bars and stores.

Baring all for beads

The first parade throws appeared in 1871, lobbed at spectators by a member of the Twelfth Night Revelers dressed as Santa Claus. By the early 1900s riders were slinging ribbons, confetti, and glass beads as a matter of course, the crowds jostling and jumping in order to catch them. Nowadays, throw frenzy rages long after the parades have rumbled past, triggering a drunken flirtation ritual whereby complete strangers, usually already heavily laden with necklaces, approach each other begging to swap one string of beads for another. Over the years, the stakes have become higher – thus the gaggle of female out-of-towners on French Quarter balconies, responding to the challenge to "show your tits!" chanted by goggling street mobs by pulling up their shirts in exchange for strings of beads and roars of boozy approval. In recent years, the guys have started to join in, eagerly pulling down their pants at the slightest provocation. Especially popular among the gay boys, this practice is officially illegal – however, though stripping off Uptown, where carnival is more of a family affair, is certainly a no-no, in the French Quarter pretty much anything goes. New Orleanians leave these antics to the tourists: anyone desperate to see (or join) the show should head for Bourbon Street – a tacky strip at the best of times, and sheer mayhem during Mardi Gras.

six or seven miles and can take at least three hours to pass any one point, their multi-tiered floats joined by the city's famed high-school marching bands – whose ear-splitting blast of drums and brass can be heard for miles – along with weirdly masked horsemen, stilt walkers, and the Second Liners who dance behind. Night parades may also be accompanied by black flambeaux carriers, whose nerve-wracking swirling and leaping is rewarded by a scattering of quarters thrown by the crowds.

Visitors who don't fancy scrabbling on the sidewalk for plastic trinkets pay for places on stands, often linked to a hotel or restaurant, where $15 or so gets you a good view and an elevated vantage point for catching throws. In the less congested areas outside downtown, families colonize whole swathes of sidewalk with picnic boxes, folding chairs, and stepladders. Others hop around, dipping in and out of side streets to catch up and overtake the rumbling floats. Good viewing areas include Canal Street, which sees the densest crowds, and St Charles Avenue, especially between First and Jackson, where there's more of a local scene. Bear in mind when staking your place that parade schedules tend to be approximate – Zulu, in particular, who parades first thing on Mardi Gras day, is notorious for setting off two or three hours late.

Participating in a parade

While marveling at a particularly inventive, elaborate, or just plain funny float (and bitching about the lame ones) is part of the fun, most are here to do more than just watch. Everyone, from the wiry, hyper kids with jabbing elbows to the fierce old ladies hovering above the crowds on customized stepladders, are out to catch "throws," be they strings of beads, fluffy toys, beakers, toys, or doubloons (tin coins marked with krewe insignia). Once the towering float-riders start throwing, the leaping and screaming and begging ("Throw me somethin' mista! Throw me somethin'!") begins, and the krewe members milk the hysteria for all it's worth, teasing and taunting the hoi polloi below them. Souvenirs vary in worth: the bright, cheap strings of beads that adorn balconies everywhere are the most common, while Zulu's spears and coconuts – handed out rather than thrown – have become the most treasured. While old-guard krewes – including Rex – tend to be more restrained with their throws, the super krewes are the most excessive. Endymion float-riders, in particular, shower the streets with bagfuls of fat beads, perilous towers of plastic beakers, and a rainstorm of doubloons.

Lundi Gras

The day before Mardi Gras, Lundi Gras is one of the liveliest of the season. Things formally get going at 10.30am, when some of the city's best performers, most of whom will have been gigging till daybreak for the past two weeks, play at Zulu's free riverside music festival at Woldenberg Park. After a few hours relaxing on the grass, snacking on fried

chicken and cold beer, listening to fine R&B, jazz, and blues, at 5pm it's time to leap up again to see Zulu's king and queen arrive by boat. When they've disembarked, you can head just around the corner to the Plaza d'España, where at 6pm, in a formal ceremony unchanged for more than a century, the mayor hands the city to Rex, King of Carnival. Everyone cheers, and the businessman in the golden robes, page-boy wig, and false beard shakes his scepter graciously. A ceremonial meeting between Zulu and Rex ensues, followed by big-name bands and fireworks. From there people head off for the Proteus and Orpheus parades or to embark on yet another frenzied evening of live music. Most clubs are still hopping well into Mardi Gras morning.

Mardi Gras

The fun starts early on Mardi Gras day, when marching clubs, made up of local musicians, writers, and sundry barflies, stride through uptown on their ritualized bar crawls. Meanwhile, on the other side of town, the resplendent Mardi Gras Indians gather to parade, preparing for their afternoon standoffs. The Backstreet Cultural Museum (see p.116) and *Ernie K-Doe's Mother-in-Law Lounge* (p.119) are good places to hang out, as many Indians, Skeletons, Baby Dolls, and other black Tremé groups drop by before and during their parades. Zulu, scheduled to set off at 8.30am – but usually starting much later – heads from

▼ KING CAKE

Uptown to Canal Street, its float-riders daubed in war paint and dressed in grass skirts. Their wild burlesque is trailed by the motley Krewe du Julu walking parade. One of the unofficial krewes, Julu, accompanied by klezmer music from the Olympia Brass Band, finds new ways each year to illegally infiltrate the official parade routes; how far they get depends upon when the police eventually catch up with them. Following Zulu, the refined Rex parade, dominated by the colossal Boeuf Gras – a fatted calf, symbolizing the last flesh before fasting – hits Canal Street in the afternoon. Ironically, by the time Rex turns up, most people have had their fill of the official parades. The wildest party is going on in the French Quarter, which is teeming with masked, costumed merrymakers, bead-strung tourists, strutting drag divas, tit-flashing teens, and banner-carrying Baptists preaching hellfire and brimstone. Most of the action is on the streets – indeed, many bars and restaurants close for the day – but some restaurants offer special packages whereby $50 or so gets you a day pass that includes food, drink, and, crucially, use of the restrooms.

Though it's best to do as most people do and drift through the maelstrom, there are a couple of high points to know about. The surreal St Ann walking parade, a stunning procession of the most extraordinary costumes, gathers in the Bywater and hits the Quarter at around 11am, usually stopping for drinks at the *R-Bar* (see p.110) before marching down Royal Street to Canal. Anyone is welcome to prance through the streets with them; you'll fit in best if your costume is wild, beautiful, or creative. Meanwhile, on the corner of St Ann and Bourbon, the outrageous gay costume competition known as the Bourbon Street Awards gets going at noon. This is one to watch rather than join – unless, of course, you're a drag queen who has just happened to wander by in a twenty-foot-high sequinned seahorse ensemble.

Late afternoon, hipsters head to the Faubourg, where Frenchmen Street is ablaze with bizarrely costumed carousers and drummers. The fun continues throughout the Quarter and the Faubourg until midnight, when a siren wail heralds the arrival of mounted police who sweep through Bourbon Street and declare through megaphones that carnival is officially over. Some bars do stay open later, but most people, masks askew, are drifting home by 1am. Like all good Catholic cities, New Orleans takes carnival very seriously. Midnight marks the onset of Lent, and repentance can begin.

Accommodation

Hotels

New Orleans has some fantastic places to stay, from rambling old B&Bs to hip boutique hotels in restored historic buildings. It's well worth budgeting to pay a bit more to stay in the French Quarter, in the heart of things. Many accommodations here are in guesthouses, most of them in old Creole cottages or townhouses, furnished with antiques. These are some of the most beautiful lodgings in the city, ranging from shabbily decadent places with iffy plumbing to romantic honeymooners' hideaways. Some can be dark and a little musty inside – in the Creole tradition, they're shaded from the heat, sun, and rain by lush patios and cranky wooden shutters – but many also have courtyards, balconies, verandas, and pools. Most serve continental breakfast, and in the more expensive places you may also get complimentary evening drinks and hors d'oeuvres. Very few places in the Quarter offer free parking – you can pay as much as $25 per night to park – so if you're driving you may do better to leave your car in one of the lots down by the river for the duration.

The funky Faubourg Marigny specializes in friendly, affordable B&Bs, while the Lower Garden District offers a handful of budget options near the streetcar line. For something a bit fancier, head for the Garden District proper and Uptown, where you'll find several gorgeous old places in historic buildings. The

Booking a room

Room rates, never low (you'll be pushed to find anything half decent for less than $60), increase considerably for Mardi Gras, Jazz Fest, and the Sugar Bowl, when prices can go up by as much as 200 percent. At other times, and especially during summer, when things slow down, it's worth asking about special deals. Guesthouse owners, especially, are often more willing to negotiate prices than let rooms go empty. It is also *always* worth logging onto individual hotel websites, where, all year-round, depending upon the state of the tourist industry, you might well find prices lower than their standard quoted rates. (Always phone the hotel to double-check that's the rate you'll be actually paying.)

New Orleans is not a city where you want to be stranded without a room, and though it's possible to take a chance on last-minute deals, you should ideally make reservations well in advance. This is especially true during the big festivals and special events, as well as on weekends throughout the year. Note that many places, especially in the Quarter, have minimum stays of two nights on weekends – longer during special events.

If you do turn up without a reservation, head immediately for the information center on Jackson Square (see p.188), which has racks of discount leaflets offering savings on same-day bookings (weekdays only).

Rates shown here are the standard prices quoted by the hotels, and refer to the least expensive double rooms available between October and May outside of festival times. Where places offer a choice of rooms with shared and private baths, we have quoted the cheapest room *with* bath. Unless otherwise stated the costs shown do not include the room tax, which varies between 11 and 13 percent.

Central Business District (CBD) and Warehouse District are the domain of the city's boutique and chain hotels, catering mostly to conventioneers – unless you hook a special deal, you can usually find better value elsewhere.

The French Quarter

A Creole House 1013 St Ann St at Burgundy ☎504/524-8076 or 1-800/535-7858, ◎www.acreolehouse.com. Unfussy guesthouse, bordering on shabby in places, with rooms ranging from cozy nooks with shared baths to antique-filled suites. Be

▲ African-American Museum

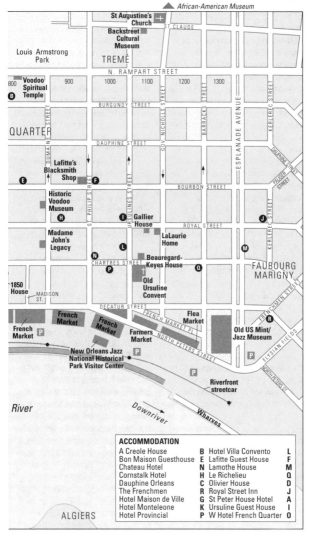

ACCOMMODATION

A Creole House	**A**	Hotel Villa Convento	**L**
Bon Maison Guesthouse	**E**	Lafitte Guest House	**F**
Chateau Hotel		Lamothe House	**N**
Cornstalk Hotel	**H**	Le Richelieu	**M**
Dauphine Orleans	**C**	Olivier House	**Q**
The Frenchmen		Royal Street Inn	**D**
Hotel Maison de Ville	**G**	St Peter House Hotel	**J**
Hotel Monteleone	**K**	Ursuline Guest House	**A**
Hotel Provincial	**P**	W Hotel French Quarter	**I**
			O

specific about what you want when making reservations and feel free to negotiate. The staff is helpful. Rates include a simple continental breakfast. From $69.
Bon Maison Guesthouse 835 Bourbon St at St Ann ☎504/561-8498, ⊛www .bonmaison.com. Set back from the road behind a brick courtyard, this Creole townhouse has been converted into a laid-back, no-fuss guesthouse. The atmosphere is wonderfully peaceful, considering its location, partly because there are just five suites, all with baths, kitchenettes, and private entrances. It's particularly popular with gay guests, but everyone is welcome. No children. Reservations essential. $95–145

for two guests, $165 for three, $175 for four, including room tax.

Chateau Hotel 1001 Chartres St at St Philip ☏504/524-9636, ⊛www .chateauhotel.com. Simple, clean rooms in the quieter part of the Quarter. All rooms are comfortable, but some are better than others, so if you feel yours is too small or a bit dark, check to see what else is available. There's an outdoor café bar by the pool, and rates include continental breakfast (which you can have in your room). Free valet parking. Rates from $99.

Cornstalk Hotel 915 Royal St at Dumaine ☏504/523-1515, ⊛www .cornstalkhotel.com. Casually elegant place in a turreted Queen Anne house surrounded by a landmark cast-iron fence decorated with fat cornstalks. The appealing, high-ceilinged rooms are each individually furnished with antiques and feature plenty of period detail; they vary considerably in size, but all have showers, and four have baths. Continental breakfast (8–11am) can be taken in your room, on the balcony, or on the impressive front veranda overlooking Royal Street. Two-night minimum at weekends. $15 per night parking fee. $75–185.

Dauphine Orleans 415 Dauphine St at Conti ☏504/586-1800 or 1-800/521-7111, ⊛www.dauphineorleans.com. Upmarket hotel in a historic complex with more than one hundred rooms. The best are set in restored brick cottages around tranquil, lush courtyards, and have their own Jacuzzis; all of them benefit from an air-purifying system and very comfortable beds. There's a pool, a snug bar (once the site of a brothel), a guest library, and a fitness room; rates include welcome cocktails, hors d'oeuvres, a very good continental breakfast and afternoon tea. $149–309.

Lafitte Guest House 1003 Bourbon St at St Philip ☏504/581-2678 or 1-800/331-7971, ⊛www.lafitteguesthouse.com. This galleried antebellum house, on the quieter end of Bourbon, across from the historic *Lafitte's Blacksmith Shop* (see p.88), is a romantic, welcoming, gay-friendly hotel. The fourteen antique-furnished rooms vary in size and style – one of them takes up the entire top floor of the house – though all

feature original details, and many have balconies. Small touches, like the Egyptian cotton sheets, tranquil sound machines, and silk sleep masks make this place extra special. Rates include in-room continental breakfast. $179–219; $10 more at weekends.

Hotel Maison de Ville and Audubon Cottages 727 Toulouse St at Royal ☏504/561-5858, ⊛www.maisondeville .com. Ravishing small hotel, favored by Elizabeth Taylor and Tennessee Williams among others. Service is luxurious, with free evening sherry, overnight shoeshine, and continental breakfast brought to your room. The on-site *Bistro* (see p.89) is classy and secluded. There are five rooms in the main building, but they're small, so try instead for one of the nine around its stunning courtyard and turtle-filled fountain – they're smallish, too, but the setting is gorgeous. If you're after even more space try the secluded *Audubon Cottages*, a block away on Dauphine Street, with living areas, courtyards, and, in some cases, two bedrooms; there's also a pretty pool. Two-night minimum stay over weekends, and no children under 12 allowed. Weekday rates start at $195–325, *Audubon Cottages* from $225; weekends see an increase of $30–140, depending on the room.

Hotel Monteleone 214 Royal St at Iberville ☏504/523-3341 or 1-800/535-9595, ⊛www.hotelmonteleone.com. This handsome hotel, the oldest in the city, is a literary landmark, having hosted a fine array of writers and artists since 1886. At 16 stories, and with more than 600 rooms, it's something of a giant on Royal, but manages to keep its distinctive character with a handsome baroque facade, elegant marble lobby, and revolving bar. Rooms are very comfortable, too. There's a gym, heated rooftop pool, and a beauty salon; they also offer a baby-sitting service. Rates from $150.

Olivier House 828 Toulouse St at Bourbon ☏504/525-8456, ⊛www .olivierhouse.com. Quintessentially New Orleans hotel in three handsome Creole townhouses with a warren of corridors, balconies, and stairwells. Like many of the Quarter's oldest establishments, it can feel a bit dark, but it's immensely atmospheric and very good value. The 42 rooms (all with baths and kitchenettes) vary, but most of them are appealingly old-fashioned, with funky antique furniture, chandeliers, and tall, shuttered windows. If money's no object, go for the garden suite, which has its own internal garden and fountain. Other rooms have small patios. There's a tropical courtyard, and a tiny pool. Free parking (a rarity in French Quarter hotels) in a small lot nearby. From $99.

Hotel Provincial 1024 Chartres St at Ursulines ☏504/581-4995 or 1-800/535-7922, ✇www.hotelprovincial.com. With nearly one hundred rooms, this sprawling – yet somehow intimate and relaxed – place is set in a quiet part of the Quarter, with rooms opening onto five peaceful, gaslit courtyards. Some rooms are filled with antiques, others are more ordinary. There are two nice outdoor pools (but avoid rooms nearby if you want a bit of peace), a bar, a coffee bar, and a fancy restaurant on site. No breakfast, though, and valet parking costs $15 per night. Booking in advance through the website gets you good deals, and if you turn up without a reservation you may find leaflets offering weekday rates as low as $69–89 in the tourist office (see p.188), but the standard rates hover around $99–199.

Le Richelieu 1234 Chartres St at Barracks ☏504/529-2492 or 1-800/535-9653, ✇www.lerichelieuhotel.com. Handsome hotel in a restored factory and neighboring townhouse. Though the old-world ambience of the lovely lobby is not continued in the rooms, they are nonetheless comfortable and attractive, with all mod cons. There's a small outdoor pool overlooked by a café serving light meals and coffee, free local calls, and free on-site parking. They also offer a baby-sitting service. Rates from $100.

St Peter House Hotel 1005 St Peter St at Burgundy ☏504/524-9232 or 1-888/604-6226, ✇www.stpeterhouse.com. Historic building with 29 darkish, spacious, comfortable rooms – some set around a courtyard, others with access to the wrap-around balcony – popular with a mixed gay and straight clientele. Though it's certainly basic – and can be noisy if you're staying at the front – it's clean and efficiently run. Rates include minimal continental breakfast. $49–199; $10 more at the weekend.

Ursuline Guest House 708 Ursulines St at Royal ☏504/525-8509 or 1-800/654-2351. No young children are allowed at this modest place, which caters to a mixed gay and straight clientele. The twelve rooms, all with baths, open onto a broad gallery or the courtyard (which, though rather ordinary, does have a Jacuzzi); those with window air-conditioners can be noisy. Rates include continental breakfast and evening drinks. There are three parking spaces, at $10 each per night. $95–125.

Hotel Villa Convento 616 Ursulines St at Chartres ☏504/522-1793, ✇www.villaconvento.com. It's not the original House of the Rising Sun, whatever the buggy-drivers might tell you, but a friendly, family-run place with the feel of an old European boarding house. Rates are low for the Quarter, and it's often booked with return visitors. The public spaces are getting rather shabby, but the twenty-five no-frills rooms with baths are clean and comfortable; some have very small balconies. Complimentary continental breakfast served in the courtyard from 7–10am. Parking $7. $99–175; no increase at weekends.

W Hotel French Quarter 316 Chartres St at Bienville ☏504/581-1200, ✇www.whotels.com. Smaller and slightly less pretentious than its CBD counterpart (see p.180), this boutique branch of the *W* chain offers the same concept, with stylish rooms, a trendy bar, the *Living Room*, in-room CD- and video-players, and a dash of local flavor in the New Orleans courtyard. Despite the style, however, this is really a business hotel, affordable for expense-account travellers only. There's a gorgeous dark blue pool and a superb nouvelle Italian restaurant, *Bacco*, on site (see p.74). Rates from $130.

Faubourg Marigny

The Frenchmen 417 Frenchmen St at Decatur ☏504/948-2166 or 1-800/831-1781, ✇www.frenchmenhotel.com. Popular, gay-friendly guesthouse in a great location across from the Old US Mint. It is spread across two 1860 townhouses overlooking a patio; the 27 rooms, all with baths, are of varying styles and standards – nothing very fancy. There's a small pool and a Jacuzzi. Rates include continental breakfast. Rooms from $59, suites from $89, $10 more at weekends.

Lamothe House 621 Esplanade Ave at Chartres ☎504/947-1161 or 1-800/367-5858, ⊛www.lamothehouse.com. Eleven rooms and nine suites in a comfortable, shabbily elegant Victorian guesthouse. Rooms vary – those in the former slave quarters are very small indeed – but rates are usually low. There's free on-site parking, a shady pool, and free afternoon sherry and continental breakfast (served till 10.30am). Their sister property, *Marigny Guest House* (same phone and web address), in a Creole cottage on Kerlerec Street, is smaller, cheaper, and less appealing. From $69.

Royal Street Inn 1431 Royal St at Kerlerec ☎504/948-7499 or 1-800/449-5535, ⊛www.royalstreetinn.com. Hip lodging above the funky *R-Bar* (see p.110), and run by the same people. The six, good-looking, clean rooms (all with baths) are decorated on themes ranging from Art Deco to bordello; those for two people are small-ish; the larger four-person "Ghost in the Attic" suite with kitchenette is good value. It's favored by a young crowd who hang out in the bar; rates include two drinks per night. No guests under 21 years allowed. From $90.

CBD and Warehouse District

International House 221 Camp St at Gravier ☎504/553-9550 or 1-800/633-5770, ⊛www.ihhotel.com. Contemporary boutique hotel in a beautifully restored Beaux Arts bank building that changes its decor to fit in with the season or the latest festival. Beyond the swish design, the very beige guest rooms are comfortable, filled with books about the city, jazz CDs, and photos of musicians. The lobby bar can get noisy. Rates include continental breakfast. Parking $26 per night. From $180.

La Salle Hotel 1113 Canal St at Basin ☎504/523-5831 or 1-800/521-9450. Budget option wedged between the Saenger Theater and an old-fashioned wig shop, on the border of the Quarter and Tremé. Absolutely no frills beyond free coffee and donuts, just plain rooms – some with baths. The public spaces are a bit shabby, and non-smokers might find the full ashtrays a bit of a problem, but staff is friendly and the prices are good. The area can feel unsafe at night, so doors are locked from 11pm. Rates from $50.

Hotel Monaco 333 St Charles Ave at Perdido ☎504/561-0010, ⊛www .monaco-neworleans.com. High-concept boutique hotel, housed in a handsome 1926 Masonic temple, which, despite its leopard-spotted robes, African art, funky faux fur throws, and pet goldfish on request, is basically a dressed-up business hotel. Even so, it's got a reputation for occasional water pressure/temperature hitches, so ask for a room with no plumbing problems. Amiable staff mingle with guests during the daily free wine tastings (5–6pm), when you can also get a free five-minute back rub. No pool, but there is a gym. Valet parking $29 per night. Rates from $150.

The Pelham Hotel 444 Common St at Magazine ☎504/522-4444 or 1-888/856-4486, ⊛www.thepelhamhotel .com. Mid-range hotel in a nineteenth-century building, facing a homeless shelter, conveniently located a couple of blocks from Canal Street. It's a low-key place, with comfortable, attractive rooms; rates vary widely, but are generally cheaper at the weekends. $8 per night is added to the room rate for the personal safe and unlimited local and long-distance calls. From $69.

W Hotel 333 Poydras St at S Peters ☎504/525-9444 or 1-800/622-5953, ⊛www.whotels.com. From the outside, this is just another CBD tower: inside, the slick, über-designed public spaces, including bar, are scuttling with fashion slaves and stressed-out business folk. If you prefer New York style and attitude – haughty service, hip furnishings, and super-cool fellow guests – to rough-hewn New Orleans charm, you'll love the *W*. Rates from $130.

Lower Garden District

HI-New Orleans Marquette House 2249 Carondelet St at Jackson ☎504/523-3014. New Orleans' only official hostel lies a block from the streetcar line. It's not one of the nicest HI properties, with so-so communal areas, but prices are low. Dorm beds go for $18–21; there are double rooms, a few with kitchens, in a separate building. The crowd is slightly older than at the city's other hostels – there's a ban on alcohol. Day use allowed and no curfew. Reservations recommended. Rooms $55.

McKendrick-Breaux House 1474 Magazine St at Race ☎504/586-1700 or 1-888/570-1700, ☎www.mckendrick-breaux.com. Lovely B&B with just nine rooms in a restored nineteenth-century home. The large, antique-filled rooms are prettily decorated with fresh flowers and original paintings; all have baths (clawfoot tubs abound) and some feature balconies overlooking the patio (which has a Jacuzzi). Rates include a good continental breakfast, served by the knowledgeable, personable hosts. Free off-street parking. Rates from $135.

Prytania Park 1525 Prytania St at Terpsichore ☎504/524-0427 or 1-800/862-1984, ☎www.prytaniaparkhotel.com. Peaceful hotel with a varied selection of historic and modern rooms, including lofts that sleep four or five. All rooms have fridges and microwaves; rates include a simple continental breakfast, which you can eat in the small courtyard. Parking $10. Standard rates from $69; the tourist office (see p.188) usually has brochures detailing weekday discounts.

St Charles Guest House 1748 Prytania St at Polymnia ☎504/523-6556, ☎www.stcharlesguesthouse.com. This bohemian guesthouse offers a variety of rooms (all non-smoking), none with TV or phone (there's a public phone in the lobby). Rooms come with or without baths; the basic 6ft by 8ft "cabins" (first come, first served) are the cheapest option, but for the priciest en-suite doubles you can get better value elsewhere. It's friendly enough, though, with a hostel-like atmosphere, a pool, and a simple continental breakfast. They ask for deposits with reservations. From $75 for a room with a bath; cabins $35.

St Vincent's Guest House 1507 Magazine St at Race ☎504/523-3411, ☎www.stvincentsguesthouse.com. More than seventy budget rooms in a huge 1861 orphanage. The atmosphere is cheery, if institutional, and there's a pool (not always clean) – but don't expect luxury. Rates from $60.

The Garden District

Garden District Hotel 2203 St Charles Ave at Jackson ☎504/566-1200 or 1-800/205-7131, ☎www.gardendistricthotel.com. This is a standard *Ramada* property, nothing special from the outside, but reliable and comfortable, and in a great location – the St Charles streetcar stops right outside. The popular restaurant *Lulu's in the Garden* (see p.142) is on site. Rates vary considerably; always check the website for special deals and promotions. From $70.

Josephine Guest House 1450 Josephine St at Prytania ☎504/524-6361, ☎www.josephine.us. Superb guesthouse in a gorgeous 1870s home set on the fringes of the Garden District, a block away from the streetcar. The six exquisite rooms are decorated with unusual antiques and Baroque flourishes; each has a private bath and most have a balcony. Continental breakfast comes with fresh orange juice, warm biscuits, and café au lait, while drinks are served in the parlor. Discounts available in summer. $115–165.

Pontchartrain Hotel 2031 St Charles Ave at Josephine ☎504/524-0581 or 1-800/777-6193, ☎www.pontchartrainhotel.com. Though time is taking its toll on the once-grand decor of this landmark building, it's still popular with visiting dignitaries and privacy-seeking celebs (Tom Cruise and Nicole Kidman canoodled here in happier days). The guest rooms are shabbier than the public spaces, but the location – on the fringes of the Garden District – is great, and the sophisticated bar, with its dark wood and romantic corners, remains a local favorite. From $79.

Uptown

Columns Hotel 3811 St Charles Ave at General Taylor ☎504/899-9308 or 1-800/445-9308, ⓦwww.thecolumns .com. Wonderfully atmospheric hotel in an 1883 Italianate mansion. Standing in for a Storyville bordello in the 1977 movie *Pretty Baby*, the whole place seeps louche glamour, especially the faded Victorian bar and the veranda with its stately namesake columns, both of which are essentials on any drinking itinerary. The twenty rooms vary widely, but all have hardwood floors and antique furnishings; some are decorated on themes, some come with four-poster beds, others have balconies and fabulous views of St Charles Avenue. There are no TVs, and 13 rooms have showers only, with no tub. Complimentary continental breakfast, along with free copies of the

Park View Guest House

ACCOMMODATION

Columns Hotel	B	McKendrick-Breaux House	O
Garden District Hotel	H	Pelham Hotel	F
HI-New Orleans		Pontchartrain Hotel	I
Marquette House	G	Prytania Park	K
Hotel Monaco	D	St Charles Guest House	M
International House	E	St Charles Inn	C
Josephine Guest House	L	St Vincent's Guest House	N
La Salle Hotel	A	W Hotel	J

0   500 yds

Times-Picayune, are taken in a little tearoom. Rates increase enormously at Mardi Gras, owing to the hotel's prime parade-viewing location on the Avenue. $110–180.

Park View Guest House 7004 St Charles Ave at Walnut ☎504/861-7564, ☯www .parkviewguesthouse.com. Built for the 1884 Cotton Exposition, this 22-room guesthouse on the edge of Audubon Park has a lived-in feel, with lofty ceilings,

mismatched antique furniture, hardwood floors, and a roomy veranda. The rooms, some with shared baths, are comfortable, if a little chintzy; many have balconies and offer views of the park. Rates include simple continental breakfast. From $69.

St Charles Inn 3636 St Charles Ave at Foucher ☎504/899-8888 or 1-800/489-9908, ☯www.stcharlesinn.com. Old-fashioned hotel with sizeable and

India House Hostel

Canal Street streetcar

Superdome

New Orleans Arena

Public Library

City Hall

New Orleans Center

Post Office

Church of the Immaculate Conception

Union Passenger Terminal

C B D

FRENCH QUARTER

Gallier Hall

Custom House

Lee Monument

13 Sisters

St. Patrick's

Canal Place Mall

LOWER

Confederate Museum
D-Day Museum

Ogden Museum of Southern Art

CAC

Louisiana Children's Museum

Casino

GARDEN

Coliseum Square

WAREHOUSE DISTRICT

World Trade Center

Aquarium

DISTRICT

PLAZA D'ESPAÑA

Canal Street Ferry to Algiers

Riverwalk Mall

Convention Center

Riverfront streetcar

Cruise Ships

Mississippi River

Downriver

ALGIERS

Robin Street Wharf

N

– – – St. Charles streetcar
········· Riverfront streetcar
—— Canal Street streetcar

good-value, if unexciting, rooms in a prime location just beyond the Garden District, right by the streetcar stop. There's a communal lounge, and rates include continental breakfast taken in your room. Free covered parking. $100.

Mid-City

India House Hostel 124 S Lopez St at Canal ☎504/821-1904, ₩www

.indiahousehostel.com. Funky, somewhat run-down backpackers' hostel a little off the beaten track. Owned and run by keen travelers, it's the friendliest – and booziest – of the city's hostels, with a resident grumpy cat, TV, video, and Playstation, and regular rowdy pool parties. Accommodation is in two- or four-bed dorms, or a few basic rooms with shared baths. The area isn't great at night. Dorms $18; rooms from $35.

Essentials

Arrival

Millions of visitors arrive in New Orleans each year, most of them on one of the many domestic flights from the major US hubs. You can also get to the city by bus or train, but the stations aren't in a great part of town. Driving to New Orleans, while convenient, is not necessarily the easiest option – you won't be using a car much during your stay, and it costs a lot to park.

By air

Louis Armstrong International Airport (MSY), some eighteen miles northwest of downtown on I-10, has an information booth (daily 8am–9pm) in the baggage claim area, along with hotel courtesy phones.

The best way to get into town is by taxi. Flat-rate fares to downtown – a twenty- to thirty-minute journey – are $28 for up to two people, or $12 each for three or more. Simply join the line outside baggage claim and wait for the controller to usher you into a cab. If you're traveling alone, it's cheaper to take the airport shuttle (every 15min; $13 to downtown hotels, $12 each for two or more people; ☎504/522-3500), but because it stops frequently to drop people off, the journey can take longer than an hour. Tickets are available from 24-hour desks in the baggage claim area or from the driver.

By car

New Orleans is traversed by I-10, which runs east–west between Florida and California. You can get onto it from I-59 (east of the city) and I-55 (west). Taking I-12, which runs east–west north of the lake, hooks you up with the Lake Pontchartrain Causeway – at 23 miles, the longest bridge in the world – which enters the city from the northwest and connects with I-10.

Approaching from either direction on I-10 you're confronted with the usual bewildering choice of lanes and lack of signs: make sure not to stray onto I-610, which bypasses downtown altogether. For the CBD take exit 234C, following signs for the Superdome; for the French Quarter take 235B, following signs for Vieux Carré; and for the Garden District take the St Charles Street exit.

By bus or train

Greyhound buses arrive next to Amtrak at the Union Passenger Terminal, 1001 Loyola Ave, near the Superdome. This area, in the no-man's-land beneath the elevated Pontchartrain Expressway, is not particularly safe, especially at night; call a cab (see p.190) in advance to come and meet you.

Directions in New Orleans

One of New Orleans' many nicknames is "the Crescent City", because of the way it nestles between the southern shore of Lake Pontchartrain and a dramatic horse-shoe bend in the Mississippi River. This unique location makes the city's layout confusing, with streets curving to follow the river and shooting off at odd angles to head inland. In the face of such dizzying geography, compass points are of little use – locals refer instead to lakeside (toward the lake) and riverside (toward the river), and, using Canal Street as the dividing line, uptown (or upriver) and downtown (downriver).

Safety

Though statistics show that it is gradually dropping, New Orleans' high crime rate should still be taken very seriously. Most gun crimes occur in neighborhoods where tourists would simply never go, but widespread poverty and attendant drug problems do mean that simply crossing the street could take you from a familiar environment into a bleak, potentially threatening neighborhood.

While visitors who use a modicum of common sense will probably face nothing threatening, you do need to keep your wits about you. It's safe to walk around the French Quarter during the day, but be on your guard in the quieter fringes late at night, especially when approaching Rampart Street, the border with the underprivileged neighborhood of Tremé. Though you're not necessarily in any danger here – there are a number of bars and clubs along the street ensuring it is usually well-used – it can feel intimidating until you get your bearings, and Louis Armstrong Park should certainly be avoided at night. The Garden District is safe during the day – and there's little reason to be wandering around at night – but walking through parts of the Lower Garden District, including some run-down stretches on and around lower Magazine Street, can feel a little menacing at any time, though again this can be due to unfamiliarity more than anything else.

Wherever you are, if you feel nervous, trust your instincts, turn back, or call a taxi (see p.190). And always take a cab when traveling any distance outside the Quarter at night.

Information

Before you leave home, it's worth contacting the New Orleans CVB (☎1-800/672-6124, ⊛www.neworleanscvb.com), whose website is full of helpful information including printable maps. Once you've arrived, the best information, including self-guided walking tours, free maps, and a variety of discount vouchers can be found at the Welcome Center, on Jackson Square at 529 St Ann St in the French Quarter (daily 9am–5pm; ☎504/566-5031).

Useful websites

See opposite for online versions of the city's best newspapers and magazines.

⊛ **www.annerice.com**
The official site of New Orleans' quintessential horror author has more than one hundred pages, including regularly added, and very long, personal messages, all the scoop on her latest projects, and an ordering service for a range of Rice-related merchandise.

⊛ **www.eccentricneworleans.com**
A fond celebration of New Orleans' many oddballs. Read about local legends past and present, from Ruthie the Duck Lady and Evangeline the Oyster Girl to Quintron and Miss Pussycat, darlings of the performance art scene.

⊛ **www.k-doe.com**
As camp, colorful, and off the wall as the R&B legend himself, Ernie K-Doe's memorial site features a photo gallery, details of his *Mother-in-Law Lounge* (see p.119), and snippets of homespun wisdom from the "Emperor of the World" himself.

⊛ **www.mardigrasindians.com**
Detailed, well-written, and illustrated history of New Orleans' black Indians (see p.166), produced under the aegis of the Mardi Gras Indian council.

⊛ **www.mardigrasneworleans.com**
The best site on the history of Mardi Gras, including parade schedules, tips on how

ESSENTIALS City transportation

to get the most out of carnival, webcams, videos, and useful links.

🌐 **www.neworleansonline.com**
Searchable resource with copious links. Features include a directory of restaurants and hotels, with well-researched articles on culture, music, and activities. Plus Internet-only accommodation deals and download-able discount coupons.

🌐 **www.satchmo.com**
The definitive New Orleans music site, featuring listings, articles, interviews, music news, messageboards, and links to local music-related homepages.

Papers and magazines

Though New Orleans' media can be astonishingly parochial, there's no better way to get a sense of what drives this quirky city than by reading its papers. The news daily is the *Times-Picayune* (🌐www.nola.com) – a *picayune* being the Creole term for a small coin – which costs 50¢, $1.50 on Sunday. Heavily geared toward local stories, it has some strong columnists, and on Friday it includes an entertainment supplement, *Lagniappe*

(another Creole term, meaning a little extra, a treat). Literary events are listed in the books pages of the Sunday edition.

New Orleans also has a host of good free papers, available from cafés, bars, and stores. The excellent *Gambit* (🌐 www.bestofneworleans.com), pub-lished on Tuesdays, leans slightly more to the left than the *Times-Picayune*, with lively editorials and local news. Its Calendar pages are a good source of entertainment information, and foodies will appreciate the dining supplement. The student-focused monthly *Where Y'at* is worth a look for feature articles and record reviews, but star among the city's publications has to be *Offbeat* (🌐 www .offbeat.com), a splendid music monthly filled with news, features, reviews, and extensive listings. Though it's essential for info on live music, by the end of the month the listings can be less reliable, so call venues to check. *Ambush* (🌐 www .ambushmag.com), which hits the stands every other Friday, is New Orleans' major gay listings paper, available free from clubs, bars, cafés, and record stores.

WWOZ

Anyone with the slightest interest in New Orleans music should check out the fabulous, nonprofit WWOZ (90.7FM). Playing roots New Orleans music – R&B, blues, brass, jazz, funk, gospel – along with world music, Cajun, and old-time country, it also features jam sessions, interviews, poetry, and ticket competitions. You can hear it online at 🌐www.wwoz.org.

City transportation

Though New Orleans' most-visited neighborhoods are a dream to walk around, getting from one to another is not always easy on foot, and if you're traveling anywhere outside the Quarter after dark you'd do best to call a cab.

Buses and streetcars

The Regional Transit Authority (RTA; ☎ 504/248-3900, 🌐 www.norta.com)

runs a network of buses ($1.25, exact fare required; 25¢ for transfers). The most useful routes include "Magazine" (#11), which runs along Magazine Street from Canal Street to Audubon Park, and "Esplanade" (#48), which will take you from Rampart Street on the edge of the Quarter up to City Park.

You're far more likely to use the hand-some, sage green St Charles streetcar (dating back around one hundred years), which rumbles a thirteen-mile loop from the corner of Canal Street and Carondelet, along the "neutral ground" (median) of St Charles Avenue in the Garden District, past Audubon Park and the Riverbend, to Carrollton uptown ($1.25 each way; exact fare). The cars trundle along at an average speed of 9mph; it takes about 45 minutes for a full one-way trip. You may also use the handy, if less historic, bright red Canal Street streetcar, which runs from the Mississippi River, along Canal and Carrollton Avenue up to City Park ($1.25; exact fare), or the tourist-targeted Riverfront streetcar, also red, which makes ten stops between the Convention Center and Esplanade Avenue ($1.50; exact fare). This last offers a total trip of less than two miles, however, and is of most interest for the river views.

The only public transport within the French Quarter is the Vieux Carré shuttle ($1.25; exact fare) – little green buses done up to look like trolleys – which can run you into the Faubourg and the CBD.

VisiTour passes, available from the tourist office (see p.188) and most major hotels, give unlimited travel on all streetcars and buses ($5 per day, $12 for three consecutive days).

Taxis

The most convenient way of traveling any distance in New Orleans, especially after dark, is by taxi. United is by far the best firm, with the most reliable drivers and the safest cars. You can call them (℡ 504/522-9771), hail them from the street (try along Canal or Decatur), or pick them up in the French Quarter outside the *Omni Royal Orleans Hotel* on St Louis Street at Chartres.

Driving

It's not a particularly good idea to drive in New Orleans, especially around the French Quarter, where sections of the narrow, one-way streets are regularly closed off to create pedestrianized enclaves, plodding mule-drawn buggies cause traffic snarl-ups, and parking is all but impossible. Citywide, the brutal parking restrictions are something of a local joke, with a host of impenetrable regulations that lead to regular impoundments and steep fines. Meters are expensive and invariably in use, while public parking lots will charge you as much as $20 for a couple of hours. If you've arrived by car, your best bet is to stick it in the hotel parking lot – most French Quarter hotels charge for the privilege – and forget about it.

If your car is towed, call ℡ 504/565-7450. The pound is at 400 N Claiborne Ave.

Cycling

Cycling is a quick and cheap way of getting from one neighborhood to another, though the faint of heart may want to avoid the cut-throat drivers on the main roads. However, for anyone who wants to nip between the Quarter and Bywater, say, a bike can be really useful. Bicycle Michael's, in Faubourg Marigny at 622 Frenchmen St, rents road and mountain bikes (hourly $5/daily $16/weekly $75), along with locks and helmets (Mon, Tues & Thurs–Sat 10am–7pm, Sun 10am–5pm; ℡504/945-9505).

City tours

There is a bewildering variety of tours of New Orleans, from whistle-stop jaunts in air-conditioned buses to preposterous moonlit ghost-hunts. Walking tours are especially popular – notwithstanding the possibility of showers and, especially in summer, debilitating heat and humidity. The list below includes the best; the tourist office (see p.188) has racks of leaflets detailing many others.

Buggies and boats

Many visitors, especially first-timers or those with kids in tow, take a narrated trot through the Quarter, and sometimes the Faubourg, in one of the mule-drawn carriages that wait in line behind Jackson Square on Decatur. These can be fun, though in most cases you should take the "historic" running commentary with a pinch of salt – and the sight of the mules, decked out in funny hats, puts some people off. Rates are generally negotiable; expect to pay around $50 for four people for thirty to forty-five minutes.

One romantic way to while away a few hours on a steamy afternoon is to take a narrated cruise along the Mississippi. For details of the *Natchez* steamboat, and the *John James Audubon* riverboat, which travels between the aquarium and the zoo, see p.99.

Walking tours

Le Monde Creole leads very lively French Quarter walking tours, unfolding the gripping true-life saga of a wealthy Creole family – morning tours also stop at St Louis Cemetery No. 1. Meet at their store, *Le Monde Creole*, 624 Royal St (Mon–Sat 10.30am & 1.30pm, Sun 11am & 1.30pm; 2hr 30min; $20; reservations required; ☎ 504/568-1801, ⊛ www.lemondecreole.com). The *Bienville Foundation*'s walking tours emphasize the French Quarter's considerable gay history. They set off from from *Alternatives* gift store, 909 Bourbon St (Wed & Sat 1pm; 2hr–2hr 30min; $20; reservations essential; ☎ 504/945-6789). They can also offer tours on women's history, black history, writers, and jazz. For scholarly and accessible overviews of the Quarter, join the free tours offered by the *Jean Lafitte National Historical Park Service* (daily 9.30am; 1hr; free; ☎ 504/589-2133).

Space is limited, and it's first-come, first-served, so turn up after 9am at the NPS visitor center, 419 Decatur St, to collect your ticket. Friends of the Cabildo (☎ 504/523-3939) also provide reliable historical overviews, concentrating on the French Quarter. Tours set off from the 1850 House, 523 St Ann St on Jackson Square, and the cost includes admission vouchers both for the 1850 House and Madame John's Legacy, valid for three days (Mon 1.30pm, Tues–Sun 10am & 1.30pm; 2hr; $12; no reservations required, but arrive 15min early).

In recent years the choice of tours promising magic, voodoo, vampires, and ghosts has become dizzying. Among the high-camp, the overpriced, and the just plain silly, there are a few actually worth checking out. Historic New Orleans Walking Tours (☎ 504/947-2120, ⊛ www.tourneworleans.com) has a good "Cemetery/Voodoo" tour covering St Louis Cemetery No. 1, Congo Square, Marie Laveau's home, and the Voodoo Spiritual Temple (Mon–Sat 10am & 1pm, Sun 10am; meet at *Café Beignet*, 334 Royal St), and, after dark, a "Haunted French Quarter" walk, which is slightly more tongue-in-cheek (daily 7.30pm; meet at *O'Flaherty's* bar, 508 Toulouse St). The Garden District/Cemetery tour covers Lafayette Cemetery No. 1 (daily 11am & 1.45pm; meet at the *Garden District Bookshop* in the Rink mall, 2727 Prytania St). All cost $15, last around 2hr, and need no reservations; arrive 15min early. *Save Our Cemeteries* (☎ 504/525-3377, ⊛ www.saveourcemeteries.org) is a nonprofit restoration organization leading fascinating tours of Lafayette No. 1 (Mon, Wed, Fri & Sat 10.30am; 1hr; $6; meet at the Washington Avenue Gate, 1400 block of Washington Ave) and St Louis No. 1 (Sun 10am; 1hr 30min; $12; meet at the *Royal Blend* coffeeshop, 621 Royal St). No reservations are needed for either.

Festivals and holidays

As befits this party-loving, parade-crazy, multicultural city, New Orleans' calendar is packed with festivals. The big one, of course, is Mardi Gras (see p.162), closely followed by the superb Jazz Fest – for both of these be sure to reserve a hotel room well in advance – but whenever you come you're bound to coincide with some celebration or other, be it a saint's day or a sinner's beanfeast. For a full rundown, contact the New Orleans CVB (☎1-800/672-6124, ◉www.neworleanscvb.com); neighborhood events are announced on WWOZ (see p.189).

St Patrick's Day

March 17. New Orleanians start celebrating the Irish saint's day on the Friday before, with a French Quarter walking parade that sets off from *Molly's at the Market* bar (see p.67). The next day, another parade heads through the Irish Channel – the blue-collar neighborhood between the Garden District and the river – with float-riders throwing vegetables to a green-bead-clad bunch of roisterers. On March 17 itself, there's a street party in the Irish Channel, organized by *Parasol's* bar (see p.143).

St Joseph's Day/ Super Sunday

March 19. The Sicilian saint's day, roughly halfway through Lent, is a big deal in this most Catholic of cities. Massive altars of food, groaning with bread, fig-cakes, cookies, and stuffed artichokes are erected in churches all around town (including St Louis Cathedral's garden) and the French Market. During the French Quarter parade, the Saturday before, float-riders fling flowers and exchange lucky beans for kisses. The Sunday closest to St Joseph's (Super Sunday) is also the only time outside Mardi Gras that the Mardi Gras Indians parade.

Tennessee Williams Literary Festival

Late March. ☎504/581-1144, ◉www.tennesseewilliams.net. This superb five-day festival attracts a host of internationally known actors and writers to the French Quarter. Though ground zero is the *Petit Théâtre du Vieux Carré* (see p.59), many of the readings and discussions are held in local bars. The finale, the Stanley and Stella (from *A Streetcar Named Desire*) shouting contest, in which overwrought Stanleys compete

Public holidays

On the national public holidays, stores, banks, and public and federal offices are liable to be closed all day.

January
1: New Year's Day
3rd Monday: Dr Martin Luther King Jr's Birthday

February
3rd Monday: Presidents' Day

May
Last Monday: Memorial Day

July
4: Independence Day

September
1st Monday: Labor Day

October
2nd Monday: Columbus Day

November
11: Veterans' Day
4th Thursday: Thanksgiving Day

December
25: Christmas Day

Jazz Fest

The internationally acclaimed **New Orleans Jazz and Heritage Festival** (Jazz Fest) is held during the last weekend (Fri–Sun) in April and the first weekend (Thurs–Sun) in May, at the Fair Grounds racetrack near City Park. Starting small in 1969, it has mushroomed to become an enormous affair, attracting nationwide acts and rivaling Mardi Gras in size and importance. Detractors complain that it has suffered as a consequence, and that corporate sponsorship has done little to improve quality, but gripes about overcrowding (the second Thursday, traditionally one of the quietest days of the festival, before the weekenders hit town, is a favorite with locals; the second Saturday, on the other hand, has been known to draw more than 100,000 spectators) and occasional poor acoustics apart, it's still a fantastic show, attracting a mellower audience than Mardi Gras. The "jazz" of the title is taken as a loose concept, with a dozen or so stages hosting R&B, gospel, funk, blues, African, Caribbean, Latin, Cajun, folk, bluegrass, reggae, country, Mardi Gras Indian, and brass band music.

The Fair Grounds site stays open from 11am to 7pm. While some people book up for all seven days, others prefer to pace themselves; there's plenty going on in town, including free in-store performances by Jazz Fest acts at local record stores. In the evenings, in addition to the official big-name concerts, smaller clubs feature superb line-ups and unofficial jam sessions into the early hours.

Schedules are listed a couple of months in advance on the website (ⓦwww .nojazzfest.com), and during the festival itself in the *Times-Picayune*, *Gambit*, and *Offbeat*. Tickets, available from Ticketmaster (☏504/522-5555, ⓦwww.ticket-master.com), cost $20 per day; you can also buy them for $25 on the day at the Ticketmaster stand in *Tower Records* (see p.197), but you may have to wait in a long line, and they charge a handling fee. The official evening concerts, which book up fast, cost between $25 and $60. To get to the Fair Grounds, hop on a shuttle bus from downtown ($10 round-trip), or try your luck finding a taxi; they hike their rates during the festival and drop off at designated ranks near the Fair Grounds.

in Jackson Square to holler "Stellaaaa!" as loudly as they can, has become a cult.

French Quarter Festival

Early April. ☏504/522-5730, ⓦwww .frenchquarterfestivals.org. This lively free music festival has come to rival Jazz Fest for the quality and variety of local roots music – brass, R&B, Latin, jazz – on offer. For three days the Quarter is even more vibrant than usual, with stages and food stalls along Royal and Bourbon streets, in Jackson Square and Woldenberg Park, plus parades, workshops, tours, and fireworks.

Essence Music Festival

Early July. ☏504/523-5652, ⓦwww .essence.com. Major black music festival, held in the Superdome, that brings in visitors from around the country for three days of big-name performers.

Satchmo SummerFest

End July/early Aug. ☏504/522-5730, ⓦwww.frenchquarterfestivals.org. Free five-day festival celebrating Louis Armstrong's birthday. Talks and exhibits, staged at the US Mint (see p.62), focus on the heritage of Satchmo himself, while at the weekend local jazz and brass bands play live. Plus parades, special gigs, and a jazz mass in Tremé's St Augustine's church.

Southern Decadence

On and around Labor Day (first weekend of Sept). ⓦ www.southerndecadence .com. New Orleans' biggest gay extravaganza, held over six days, brings more than 120,000 party animals to the gay bars and clubs of the French Quarter. Cocktail parties, wet boxers contests and block parties abound, with an unruly costume parade of thousands on the Sunday afternoon.

Swampfest

First two weekends of Oct. ☎504/581-4629, ⊛ www.auduboninstitute.org/swampfest. Terrific free music festival held at Audubon Zoo. Celebrating the culture of southern Louisiana, it features big-name Cajun and zydeco bands, crafts demonstrations, and some truly fantastic food stalls.

Art for Art's Sake

First Sat of Oct. ☎ 504/528-3800, ⊛ www.cacno.org. The city's major art event includes gallery receptions in the Arts District, along Magazine Street and in the French Quarter, a block party on Julia Street, and a closing gala at the CAC (see p.133).

Halloween

Oct 31. Thanks to its long-held fascination with all things morbid, and the local passion for partying and costuming, New Orleans is the perfect place to celebrate Halloween. The best public events include the wild, arty "Decadence" bash, a free party usually thrown somewhere in Bywater (look out for flyers in the hipper Faubourg and Quarter bars); the walking parade organized by *Molly's* bar in the Quarter (see p.189); and the thousands-strong masked fundraiser for Lazarus House, a local AIDS hospice (⊛www.halloweenneworleans.com). On the night itself, get dressed up and head to the Faubourg, where you'll find the scariest street party in town.

Christmas New Orleans

Dec. Though the entire city looks gorgeous during the festive season, garlanded with lights and beribboned wreaths, the French Quarter really pulls out all the stops. Events include jazz masses at the cathedral; candlelit house tours; and *prix-fixe* feasts, known as *reveillons*, put on by the finest Creole restaurants. City Park has its own festival of lights and an ice rink open for the season. ⊛www.frenchquarterfestivals.org.

Glossaries

From its hauntingly lovely Latin-influenced architecture to its long-held carnival traditions, New Orleans feels more like a Caribbean or southern European port than an American metropolis. Add to this the city's lively vernacular, peppered with words and phrases from as far away as Paris and Haiti, and its distinctive accent – a melding of French, Spanish, Irish, Sicilian, and African that, bizarrely, sounds more like Brooklynese than a Deep South drawl – and you may have to pinch yourself to remind yourself you're in the United States.

Architectural and historical terms

Banquette Sidewalk

Briquette entre poteaux Architectural process used in eighteenth-century New Orleans houses; soft brick is set between steadying, hand-hewn cypress beams.

Cajun Rural, French-speaking people living in the bayous and plains of southern Louisiana. Cajun cuisine is spicy, one-pot, country cooking; Cajun music is based around the fiddle and the accordion, with lilting lyrics sung in French.

Colonnette Narrow iron pillar holding up the gallery of a Creole townhouse.

Creole Literally, a free person descended from Spanish or French settlers in the nineteenth-century colony. It has since come to refer to anyone born in the city, including black Creoles. From the Spanish *criollo*, or native. Creole cooking is a spicy, substantial blend of French, Spanish, African, and Caribbean cuisine, mixed up with a host of other influences including Native American and Italian.

Creole cottage Typical French Quarter residence, raised from the ground above a closed, ventilated "crawl space," and with a high gabled roof. Doors open straight from the street into the living quarters, and are indistinguishable from the outside from the shuttered ceiling-to-floor windows.

Creole townhouse Multi-story version of the Creole cottage.

Fais-do-do Cajun dance.

Free people of color/Free men of color/Gens de couleur libres Educated, often wealthy, black Francophones, most of whom were slave owners from the West Indian colonies, and who, unlike the enslaved blacks, owned property and held some political power.

Gallery Outside porch, often supported on colonnettes, and extending over the sidewalk.

Garçonnière Small apartment in the courtyard of a Creole residence, where the sons of the house would live after reaching adolescence.

Gris-gris ("gree-gree") Voodoo term for a spell or totem.

Krewe Carnival club.

Neutral Ground Median.

Quadroon Nineteenth-century term to define somebody who was one-quarter black.

Quadroon balls Nineteenth-century dances, held in the Creole city (today's French Quarter), where under a formalised system known as *plaçage*, white men could take young mixed-race women as their mistresses.

Second Line Line of mourners that dances behind the brass band in a jazz funeral, often swirling frilly umbrellas; more broadly, the motley group of dancers who spontaneously attach themselves to a parade.

Shotgun cottage Long, narrow clapboard structures, built in the late 1800s, with a single row of rooms opening onto each other. Usually painted in bright or ice-cream colours, they're also notable for their decorative wooden gingerbread details.

Vieux Carré ("voo carray") Another name for the French Quarter; French for "Old Square."

Zydeco The raunchier black cousin of Cajun music; usually played fast and hard in steamy dancehalls.

Food and drink terms

Andouille ("on-*doo*-we") Spicy pork sausage, often in gumbo.

Bananas Foster Flamboyant dessert invented at *Brennan's* restaurant. Sliced bananas, doused in rum and banana liqueur, are added to a mountain of brown sugar and set alight at your table to create the ultimate in boozy comfort food.

Barbecue shrimp Not BBQ as we know it; the shrimp are baked in their shells and served in a buttery, garlicky sauce.

Beignets ("*ben*-yay") Deep-fried, square doughnuts without a hole, served hot and smothered in powdered sugar.

Biscuits Sourmilk scones, traditionally eaten at breakfast.

Boudin Spicy Cajun sausage of pork, liver, crawfish, and dirty rice.

Bread pudding Gooey dessert, made with French bread and raisins, and usually drenched in sweet, liquor-filled custard.

Café brûlot Dark, spicy coffee flavored with brandy, orange liqueur, orange peel, and spices, set alight before serving.

Chicory Related to endive; a roasted, ground root used to flavor New Orleans coffee.

Chitlins Smoked, savory pig intestines – delicious soul food.

Debris Juicy meat leftovers, usually from slow-cooked roast beef or pork, often served in a sloppy po-boy.

Dirty rice Rice cooked with chicken livers, giblets, onions, peppers, and spices.

Étouffé Literally "smothered" in Creole sauce (a roux with tomato, onion and spices), usually served over shrimp or crawfish on a bed of rice.

Filé Dried sassafras, formerly ground by the local Native Americans to thicken soups, and still often added to gumbo.

Grillades ("*gree*-yards") Sliced veal or beef served in a rich gravy, usually with grits, often for breakfast.

Grits Southern breakfast staple of mushy ground corn boiled and served with a dollop of butter, maple syrup, or gravy.

Gumbo Thick soup-cum-stew made with seafood, chicken, vegetables, or sausage. The name may come from *kombo*, a Native American word for filé, or *gombo*, the Bantu word for okra, which is another thickening agent.

Gumbo z'herbes Vegetarian gumbo, created by African slaves for Lent.

Hurricane Headache-inducing rum cocktail which many bars refuse to serve. It's traditionally drunk, in reckless quantities, by tourists.

Jambalaya Rice jumbled together with seafood, sausage, chicken, bell peppers, celery, and onion. The name is thought to come from the Spanish or French words for ham (*jamon* and *jambon*), tacked onto the Spanish *paella*.

King Cake A ring of sweet brioche, iced in the carnival colors of gold, green, and purple, eaten throughout Mardi Gras.

Macque choux Creamy stew of corn, tomatoes, onion, and peppers.

Mirliton Squash.

Muffuletta Italian sandwich; a sesame-seed bun stuffed with aromatic meats and cheeses, dripping with olive and garlic dressing.

Oysters Rockefeller Concocted at *Antoine's* around 1900, and named for the oil magnate. These days most versions come baked in a creamy spinach sauce, but *Antoine's* secret recipe uses greens.

Pain perdu French toast ("lost bread").

Panéed Lightly breaded and fried in butter.

Pimm's Cup The specialty of the *Napoleon House* (see p.75), served simply in a long cool glass with a slice of cucumber.

Po-boy French-bread sandwich crammed with oysters, shrimp, roast beef, or almost anything else. It was created by two local bakers in 1929, who handed them out free to striking streetcar drivers ("poor boys").

Praline ("praw-leen") Tooth-rottingly sweet candy made from caramelized brown sugar, melted butter, and pecans ("pi-*cons*").

Ramos Gin Fizz A frothy swirl of gin, lemon juice, milk, eggwhite, powdered sugar, and orange-flower water, invented by a local barman around 1900. It was later perfected at the swanky Art Deco *Sazerac Bar* (see p.125).

Ravigote Piquant mix of mayonnaise and capers, usually served with cold shellfish.

Rémoulade Chilled spicy sauce made with peppers, spring onion, horseradish, and lemon, and slathered over cold shrimp.

Roux Thickener for many Creole and Cajun sauces, made from fat and flour heated together.

Sazerac Another drink associated with the *Sazerac Bar*: a caramel-colored mix of rye whiskey, bitters, lemon, and ice, stirred together in a glass rinsed out with aniseed liqueur.

Tasso Lean, spicy smoked ham.

Directory

Alcohol The legal drinking age is 21; it's best to carry photo ID. Though 24hr drinking licenses are common, don't expect every bar to be open all night – even on Bourbon Street many places close as soon as they empty, which can be surprisingly early during slow periods. It's legal to drink in the streets, though not from a glass or a bottle – simply ask for a to-go cup from a bar and carry it with you. You'll be expected to finish it before entering another bar.

Area code ☎504.

ATMs Most of New Orleans' banks, and many of its bars, have ATMs; most accept bank cards linked to the Cirrus or Plus systems, for a fee of between $2 and, occasionally, $4 per transaction.

Cinemas Landmark Cinemas, at the Canal Place shopping mall, 333 Canal St (☎504/363-1117, ◉www.landmarktheaters.com), is a conveniently located

four-screen cinema featuring mainstream releases along with independents and world cinema. The only remaining single-screen cinema in the city is Prytania, at 5339 Prytania St at Leontine (☎504/891-2787), which shows arthouse, Hollywood, and independent movies.

Emergencies ☎911 for police, fire, and ambulance.

Internet access Access is free at the cybercafé at the CAC (see p.133). French Quarter Computer Services, 824 Chartres St, charges $2.50 for 15min rising to $30 for 5hr, along with laptop repair and printing services; they can also transfer digital camera images to CD (Mon–Fri 10am–7pm, Sat 11am–4pm; ☎504/525-4660).

Pharmacies The pharmacy at the 24hr Rite Aid, 3401 St Charles Ave (☎504/896-4575), is open 8am–11pm daily; there's also a 24-hour drive-through Walgreens at 1801 St Charles Ave (☎504/561-8458). Also Walgreens at 900 Canal St (☎504/568-1271) and in the Quarter at 134 Royal St (☎504/522-2736) and 619 Decatur St (☎504/525-7263). The Royal Pharmacy, 1101 Royal St (☎504/523-5401), is a lovely old-world place in the Quarter.

Phonecards Semans House, 115 Royal St (☎504/529-6000), sells cheap national and international phonecards.

Photo processing Avoid the cowboy outfits along Canal Street and the first blocks of the French Quarter; try Walgreens (see above, under "Pharmacies"), or French Quarter Camera, 809 Decatur St (daily 9.30am–6pm; ☎504/529-2974). If you have a digital camera, try also French Quarter Computer Services (see "Internet access" above).

Police There's a police station at 334 Royal St in the French Quarter. In emergencies call ☎911.

Post office The main post office is at 701 Loyola Ave (Mon–Fri 7am–8pm, Sat 8am–5pm, Sun noon–5pm). An equivalent service, along with fax, photocopying, FedEx, phonecards, and the like, is offered by French Quarter Postal Emporium, 1000 Bourbon St (Mon–Fri 9am–6pm, Sat 10am–3pm; ☎504/525-6651) and Royal Mail, 828 Royal St (Mon–Fri 9am–6pm, Sat 10am–4pm; ☎504/522-8523).

Tax New Orleans' sales tax is 9 percent, or 11–13 percent on hotel bills, depending on the size of the hotel. For international visitors, the Louisiana Tax-Free Shopping (LTFS) scheme reimburses the tax on all goods that you can take out of the country. Most participating businesses display a sticker; it's worth asking if you don't see one. Show your passport and they'll give you a voucher, redeemable – with the sales receipt – at the LTFS booth at the airport (Mon–Fri 7am–6pm, Sat 7am–3pm). Refunds of less than $500 are given out in cash on the spot; higher sums will be mailed. There's a small handling fee.

Tickets Ticketmaster (☎504/522-5555, ☎www.ticketmaster.com) has a booth (daily 10am–5.30pm) in *Tower Records*, 408 N Peters St.

Time New Orleans is on Central Standard Time, six hours behind Greenwich Mean Time. Daylight-Saving Time, when clocks go forward an hour, runs from the first Sunday in April to the last Sunday in October.

Tipping Wait staff in restaurants expect tips of around 17.5 percent, higher if you've had particularly good service. Bar staff should get 15 percent, or a dollar per round, whichever is higher; taxi drivers 15 percent; hotel porters about $1 per piece of baggage; and housekeeping staff $1 per night.

ROUGH GUIDES
TRAVEL SERIES

Travel guides to more than 250 destinations from Alaska to Zimbabwe

smooth travel

ROUGH GUIDES
REFERENCE SERIES

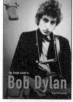

DON'T JUST TRAVEL!

Index & small print

A Rough Guide to Rough Guides

New Orleans DIRECTIONS is published by Rough Guides. The first *Rough Guide to Greece*, published in 1982, was a student scheme that became a publishing phenomenon. The immediate success of the book – with numerous reprints and a Thomas Cook prize short-listing – spawned a series that rapidly covered dozens of destinations. Rough Guides had a ready market among low-budget backpackers, but soon also acquired a much broader and older readership that relished Rough Guides' wit and inquisitiveness as much as their enthusiastic, critical approach. Everyone wants value for money, but not at any price. Rough Guides soon began supplementing the "rougher" information about hostels and low-budget listings with the kind of detail on restaurants and quality hotels that independent-minded visitors on any budget might expect, whether on business in New York or trekking in Thailand. These days the guides offer recommendations from shoestring to luxury and cover a large number of destinations around the globe, including almost every country in the Americas and Europe, more than half of Africa and most of Asia and Australasia. Rough Guides now publish:

- Travel guides to more than 200 worldwide destinations
- Dictionary phrasebooks to 22 major languages
- Maps printed on rip-proof and waterproof Polyart™ paper
- Music guides running the gamut from Opera to Elvis
- Reference books on topics as diverse as the Weather and Shakespeare
- World Music CDs in association with World Music Network

Publishing information

This 1st edition published February 2005 by **Rough Guides Ltd**, 80 Strand, London WC2R 0RL. 345 Hudson St, 4th Floor, New York, NY 10014, USA.

Distributed by the Penguin Group
Penguin Books Ltd, 80 Strand, London WC2R 0RL
Penguin Group (USA), 375 Hudson Street, NY 10014, USA
Penguin Group (Australia), 487 Maroondah Highway, PO Box 257, Ringwood, Victoria 3134, Australia
Penguin Group (Canada), 10 Alcorn Avenue, Toronto, Ontario, Canada M4V 1E4
Penguin Group (NZ), 182–190 Wairau Road, Auckland 10, New Zealand
Typeset in Bembo and Helvetica to an original design by Henry Iles.
Printed and bound in China

208pp includes index

A catalogue record for this book is available from the British Library

ISBN 1-84353-393-6

The publishers and authors have done their best to ensure the accuracy and currency of all the information in **New Orleans DIRECTIONS**, however, they can accept no responsibility for any loss, injury, or inconvenience sustained by any traveller as a result of information or advice contained in the guide.

1   3   5   7   9   8   6   4   2

Help us update

We've gone to a lot of effort to ensure that the first edition of **New Orleans DIRECTIONS** is accurate and up-to-date. However, things change – places get "discovered," opening hours are notoriously fickle, restaurants and rooms raise prices or lower standards. If you feel we've got it wrong or left something out, we'd like to know, and if you can remember the address, the price, the phone number, so much the better.

We'll credit all contributions, and send a copy of the next edition (or any other DIRECTIONS guide or Rough Guide if you prefer) for the best letters. Everyone who writes to us and isn't already a subscriber will receive a copy of our full-color thrice-yearly newsletter. Please mark letters: **"New Orleans DIRECTIONS Update"** and send to: Rough Guides, 80 Strand, London WC2R 0RL, or Rough Guides, 4th Floor, 345 Hudson St, New York, NY 10014. Or send an email to **mail@roughguides.com**

Have your questions answered and tell others about your trip at **www.roughguides.atinfopop.com**

SMALL PRINT

Rough Guide credits

Text editor: Richard Koss
Layout: Andy Hilliard
Photography: Greg Ward
Cartography: Rajesh Mishra
Picture editor: Harriet Mills

Proofreader: Diane Margolis
Production: John McKay
Design: Henry Iles
Cover art direction: Louise Boulton, Chloe Roberts

The author

Samantha Cook first visited New Orleans in 1990, fell in love with the place, and has returned every year since. She has been involved with Rough Guides for more than ten years, starting out as an author on the USA guide, and contributing to many other titles. For several years she worked in the office as an editor and managing editor, but has since returned to full-time writing.

Acknowledgments

In New Orleans, thanks to Christine de Cuir, Sal Impastato, Paul Gustings, Larone Hudson, and everyone at 500 Chartres. Thanks also to my hardworking editor, Richard Koss; Katie Lloyd-Jones, for her diligent cartographic assistance; Harriet Mills for fun picture meetings; Pam Cook; Jim Cook and Ulli Sieglohr; and of course to Greg Ward for his delightful photos, his extraordinary love and support, and, above all, his essential

Photo credits

All images © Rough Guides except the following:

p.4 French Quarter street performer © Toby Adamson/Axiom

p.11 Second line parade during Jazz Fest © Girard Mouton III/New Orleans Jazz & Heritage Festival

p.15 Preservation Hall Jazz Band © www. bighassle.com

p.16 Masked reveller at Mardi Gras © Greg Ward

p.16 Transvestites on Bourbon Street balcony © Emile D Edess/Impact Photos

p.17 Krewe of Bacchus parade © A.J. Sisco/Corbis

p.17 Mardi Gras Indian, Donald Harrison of the Creole Wild West tribe © Philip Gould/Corbis

p.17 Martina the dog, Barkus parade © David Rae Morris/Reuters/Corbis

p.17 St Ann Walking Parade © Reuters

p.25 Josephine Guest House © Josephine Guest House www.josephine.us

p.27 Pitot House © Pitot House Museum

p.31 Rue de la Course © Greg Ward

p.33 Madame John's Legacy © Greg Ward

p.36 Historic Voodoo Museum © Robert Holmes/ Corbis

p.46 New Wave Brass Band, Jazz Fest © Girard Mouton III/New Orleans Jazz & Heritage Festival

p.46 Halloween float © Apis Abramis/Alamy

p.47 French Quarter Festival © Greg Ward

p.47 Sisters of Perpetual Indulgence © Dave Fornell/Corbis

p.47 Mardi Gras Indians © Philip Gould/Corbis

p.69 Napoleon House © Greg Ward

p.162 Masked revelers © Chuck Pefley/Alamu

p.163 French Quarter balconies © Philip Gould/ Corbis

p.164 Mardi Gras float © The Image Bank/Getty Images

p.165 Bourbon Street © Greg Ward

p.167 Mardi Gras Indian © New Orleans Metropolitan Convention and Visitors Bureau, Inc./Richard Nowitz

Index

Map entries are marked in colour